DIRTY STOP OUTS GUIDE TO Coventry's Working Men's Clubs

By Ruth Cherrington

Ruth Cherrington asserts the moral right
to be identified as the author of this work.
A catalogue record for this book is available from the British Library.

Published by ACM Retro

Other titles in this series:

Dirty Stop Out's Guide to 1970s Manchester.

Dirty Stop Out's Guide to 1970s Liverpool.

Dirty Stop Out's Guide to 1970s Coventry.

Dirty Stop Out's Guide to 1970s Barnsley.

Dirty Stop Out's Guide to 1950s Sheffield.

Dirty Stop Out's Guide to 1960s Sheffield.

Dirty Stop Out's Guide to 1970s Sheffield.

Dirty Stop Out's Guide to 1980s Sheffield.

Dirty Stop Out's Guide to 1980s Sheffield – King Mojo Edition

Dirty Stop Out's Guide to 1990s Sheffield.

Dirty Stop Out's Guide to 1970s Chesterfield.

Dirty Stop Out's Guide to 1970s Sheffield – Club Fiesta Edition.

Dirty Stop Out's Guide to 1980s Chesterfield.

Dirty Stop Out's Guide to 1980s Chesterfield - Aquarius Edition.

Dirty Stop Out's Guide to 1980s Coventry.

Dirty Stop Out's Guide to 1980s Sheffield – The Limit Edition

Dirty Stop Out's Guide to 1980s Chesterfield Quizbook.

Dirty Stop Out's Guide to 1990s Chesterfield

We're on the look out for writers to cover other UK towns and cities
and we're always on the look out for great retro photos!
Please email us at **info@dirtystopouts.com** if you fancy getting involved.

www.dirtystopouts.com

DIRTY STOP OUTS GUIDE TO

Coventry's Working Men's Clubs

By Ruth Cherrington

COVENTRY'S WORKING
By Ruth Cherrington

CONTENTS

**Smiles light up
the Gas Club!
The Morgan family
on a night out**

Howitzer Club men on tour - with their beer of course!

Hen Lane Club members Bob Arnott and Will Cowburn

COVENTRY -
QUEEN OF CLUBS CITY!

Games Room get-together!

QUEEN OF CLUBS
WINS ALL HEARTS!

The city's moniker was well-earned! Around 60 working men's and social clubs were at the heart of Coventry's post-war leisure time boom offering great amenities and activities.

The city was proud to have one of the country's very first clubs: Coventry Working Men's Club, set up in 1860.

Queen Elizabeth and Prince Philip's visit to that very club in July 1977 as part of their Silver Jubilee Tour was a true first for the movement.

No reigning monarch had ever set foot inside a working men's club before and Coventry's historic club was chosen to host the royal couple. People right across the city were thrilled by this memorable event.

Queen Elizabeth's support for working men's clubs continued that shown by her great, great grandmother Queen Victoria who made a donation to the newly established Working Men's Club and Institute Union (WMCIU) in the 1860s.

Coventry clocked up 110 years of club building experience by the time Cheylesmore Social opened in 1972. It was the city's last "new" club but it had much in common with its predecessors.

Over the decades, Coventry clubs weathered many a storm including the Blitz of November 1940 and subsequent years of World War Two bombing. Clubs did their best to keep their doors open for members though several suffered serious damage and loss of life.

Above: The historic Royal visit to Coventry WMC July 1977

Barras Green Carnival Time!

★ **Barbara Weightman:**
"Working Men's Clubs were a huge part of family social life. They had bingo and entertainment of some sort too."

★ **John D'Arcy:**
"We used to go as a family to Tile Hill Club regularly back in the 1960s and 70s, usually at weekends. It was a great community club where friends met up and everyone came together. Saturdays were usually family nights. Many happy times with some great people."

After the war, Coventry achieved another first. The local authority was the first to include new working men's club in their postwar planning. They designated plots of land on rapidly developing council estates. They then took the Coventry City Bill through Parliament so that new clubs could be financed through council loans.

There was a great spirit of cooperation across the clubs with Coventry establishing its own Association of Coventry's Club Secretaries in 1944. They held their annual dinner at a different club each year with local politicians and dignitaries always in attendance.

Many local councillors were committed club members themselves and saw that people on new estates needed recreational venues. The residents happily rose to the challenge, taking up the council's offer of help to get their own clubs going.

Civic pride grew as modern Coventry, the phoenix city, emerged from the ashes with clubs part of this regeneration. Lord Mayor of Coventry in 1957, Alderman Harry Stanley believed that: "With no shadow of doubt Coventry is going to be the finest city in the country."

And so would its clubs!

Groups of ex-servicemen did what some of their predecessors did after the WW1 - came together to set up their own clubs that provided good amenities for members.

★ **Bobby Joyce:**
"My family always sat front right corner table opposite the stage door in Canley Club's concert room. My parents would send me and sister Steph down early to bag the table."

New clubs were often makeshift arrangements, with club founders using whatever they could lay their hands on. Members rolled up their sleeves to set up what quickly became home-away-from home clubs.

Their popularity can be put down to the mix of companionship, sociability, recreation and culture they provided.

By the 1970s the humble buildings of old had made way for plush concert rooms, lounges and state of the art games rooms. The growing numbers of members had rising expectations.

Club entertainment was varied with top class acts now gracing the stages.

Stanton WMC Cycling Section

The Coventry Games league had grown to be the largest in the country by the 1970s. Clubs took it in turns to host the many interclub games with coach loads turning up to play or support their teams.

Traditional games such as dominoes and snooker remained popular with others added to the mix such as golf. These all provided good company and social life, exercise and some times fresh air! The strong sense of team spirit and feelings of camaraderie were always the winners.

There were often queues outside clubs to get in before opening time. The speed with which Coventry club-goers put coats on seats and bingo pens on tables to claim their favourite seats was impressive!

★ **Mr Walrus:**
★ "My 95-year-old dad frequented many of
★ Coventry's clubs over the years. He's never
been a big drinker but he's always loved
his bingo, the fruit machines and a game of
snooker, as well as the good company."

At weekends the whole family went along, perhaps three generations strong, to enjoy the concert, bingo, perhaps a spin on the dance floor.

The clubs were a tough training ground for entertainers. Many kept their day jobs and just enjoyed taking to the stage at the weekends whilst some made it to the "big time".

Camp comedian and local man Larry "shut that

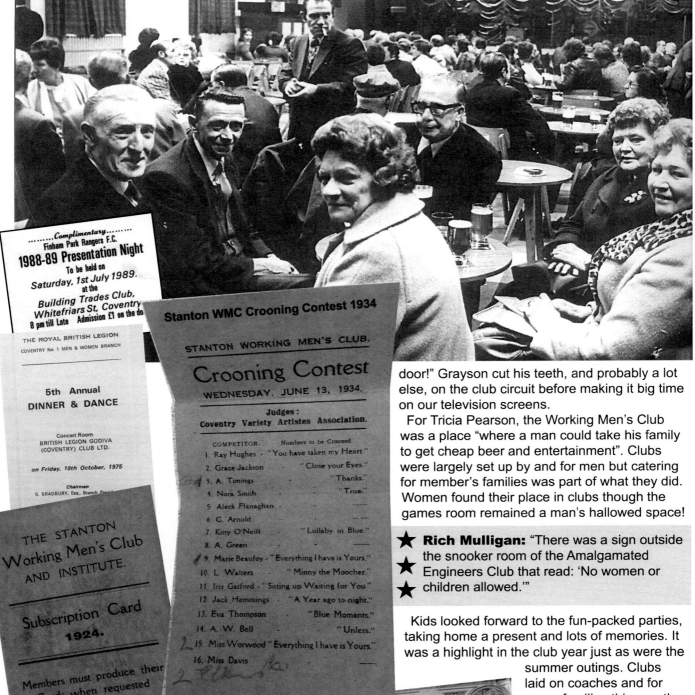

.........Complimentary.........
Finham Park Rangers F.C.
1988-89 Presentation Night
To be held on
Saturday, 1st July 1989.
at the
Building Trades Club,
Whitefriars St, Coventry
8 pm till Late   Admission £1 on the door

THE ROYAL BRITISH LEGION
COVENTRY No. 1 MEN & WOMEN BRANCH

**5th Annual
DINNER & DANCE**

Concert Room
BRITISH LEGION GODIVA
(COVENTRY) CLUB LTD.

on Friday, 10th October, 1975

Chairman
S. BRADBURY, Esq., Branch President

THE STANTON
Working Men's Club
AND INSTITUTE.

Subscription Card
1924.

Members must produce their
Cards when requested

Mr. *H Rubery*   No. **163**

Subscriptions are due the
first week in January, April, July
and October, and must be paid in
advance.

Card inspection the first
Sunday in each month.

Members one month in
arrears are not entitled to use the
club.

The Secretary's hours for
receiving Subscriptions are
Fridays, 7.30 p.m. to 9.0 p.m. ;
Sundays, 11.30 a.m. to 12.30 p.m.

1924 Quarter ending	Subs.	Lady's Ticket	C.U. Goods	Secretary's Signature
MARCH	2/.		6	ED
JUNE	4			JM
SEPT.				
DEC.	4			JM

Stanton WMC Crooning Contest 1934

STANTON WORKING MEN'S CLUB.

Crooning Contest
WEDNESDAY. JUNE 13, 1934.

Judges :
Coventry Variety Artistes Association.

COMPETITOR.	Numbers to be Crooned.
1. Ray Hughes -	"You have taken my Heart"
2. Grace Jackson	"Close your Eyes."
3. A. Timings -	"Thanks."
4. Nora Smith	"True."
5. Aleck Flanaghan -	
6. C. Arnold	
7. Kitty O'Neill	"Lullaby in Blue."
8. A. Green	
9. Marie Beaufoy -	"Everything I have is Yours."
10. L Walters -	"Minny the Moocher."
11. Iris Gatford -	"Sitting up Waiting for You"
12. Jack Hemmings -	"A Year ago to-night."
13. Eva Thompson -	"Blue Moments."
14. A. W. Bell -	"Unless."
15. Miss Worwood	"Everything I have is Yours."
16. Miss Davis	

door!" Grayson cut his teeth, and probably a lot else, on the club circuit before making it big time on our television screens.

For Tricia Pearson, the Working Men's Club was a place "where a man could take his family to get cheap beer and entertainment". Clubs were largely set up by and for men but catering for member's families was part of what they did. Women found their place in clubs though the games room remained a man's hallowed space!

★ **Rich Mulligan:** "There was a sign outside the snooker room of the Amalgamated Engineers Club that read: 'No women or children allowed.'"

Kids looked forward to the fun-packed parties, taking home a present and lots of memories. It was a highlight in the club year just as were the summer outings. Clubs laid on coaches and for some families this was the only time they went to the seaside.

Older members had their own special 'dos', such as Christmas dinners and outings. Many clubs offered discounts on their drinks and other concessions for their respected senior members.

**Subs card and
Keresley Coronation
Club Pass Card**

PAB 499278
WORKING MENS CLUB INSTITUTE UNION
KERESLEY CORONATION
OF THE
CLUB AND INSTITUTE
IS AN ASSOCIATE

ATE MUST PERSONALLY SIGN HIS NAME

Stuart Beamish joined the "Corrie" - Keresley Coronation Club- when he turned 18 and drank there until he left the area. Roy Lenton used the same club. "I used to drink and play dominoes at the Coronation Club. Happy days!"

Families celebrated most social occasions in their clubs - births, weddings and funerals. The club was often the only place for the final send-off of a loved one.

Clubs were community oriented and did a lot of charity work. You might bump into the local vicar, MP, your children's teachers all carrying out their duties in the club!

★ **Helen Reith:**

★ "We used to go to the Canley Club on New Year's Day. It was amazing, all the families gathering together. Packed to the rafters! People would arrive early, even before it opened, to get a seat."

A succession of Lord Mayors, councillors and MPs, sang the praises of the city's clubs and regularly officiated at openings of refurbished premises. They were always willing to pull the first pint- probably to drink it as well!

Recreation and entertainment were important reasons for joining clubs but they were not the only ones. Some clubs took their educational roles seriously with reading rooms and small libraries. Others even ran adult classes.

Members enjoyed a few games of "housey

housey" as bingo used to be called. Not only offering a chance for players to win prizes or a bit of money, the game also added to the clubs' coffers. Some people would visit several clubs a week chasing the "big money."

You might meet the love of your life at your local club! Prominent club official Jimmy Cooke did just that - he met his wife Flora at the Stanton Club and often commented on his fond memories of the club.

Trev Teasdel's mum met her second husband at the Willenhall Social Club. "He played accordion in a band in his free time and they did lot of popular songs in the club."

The wide range of club activities is hard to grasp now, with everything from ballroom dancing to bowls and boxing, pigeon flying and pool. You could even get a haircut! Roy Lenton's dad's mate Rex was a barber and cut hair on Monday mornings at the Coronation Club.

Margery Teasdel and George Ovington...met at the Willenhall Club in January 1980, married three months later!

Limetree Club Fishing Presentation

10 **Coventry Club Secretaries Dinner** THE CLUB AND INSTITUTE JOURNAL October, 1960

COVENTRY CLUB SECRETARIES FETED

Smiles are the order of the day at the reception given to the Coventry Club Secretaries' Association and guests by the Lord Mayor and Lady Mayoress of Coventry. Included in this photo are G. Winterburn, H. Gilmore, J Stringer, S. Porter, G. Radburn, the Lady Mayoress, Lord Mayor, Pat Ansell, R. Hudson and Arthur Bates. (See report below)

IN 1957 the 36 Clubs of the Coventry Secretaries' Association were honoured by an invitation from Alderman Pearl Hyde, M.B.E., to a Civic Reception. Now they have been honoured by an invitation to a Civic Dinner, held in the 600-year-old St. Mary's Hall by the Lord Mayor and Mayoress of Coventry, Alderman and Mrs. Harry Stanley

The Lord Mayor is a member of the Wyken W.M., Stoke Aldermoor Social, Coventry Building Trades Clubs and the new £53,000 Bell Green Club, which he played a great part in forming.

Four Officials from each of the 38 Coventry C.I U. Clubs were present Guests included the Vice-President of the Union, Arthur Bates, the Deputy Chief Constable, Mr Stanley Porter, Harry Gilmore and Pat Ansell (National Executive), George Radburn (Branch President) and Jack Stringer (Branch Secretary), Councillor E. Weaver, W Parfitt, H. Roberts and McLatchie.

Arthur Bates, proposing the toast to the City of Coventry and the Lord Mayor and Mayoress, said he had watched with pride the progress of the rebuilding of the City

Coventry had set a pattern to the rest of the country in providing sites and loaning money for the building of Clubs. He had heard of the progress from the National Member Pat Ansell, and seeing for himself, he did not think Pat had over-praised Coventry Council.

Harry Gilmore proposed the toast of the Coventry C.I U Secretaries' Association, praising their work and remarking that he knew from experience in his own Branch the good work that the Secretaries' Association did in exchanging information.

George Winterburn, the Association Vice-Chairman, replied that the Association was formed 15 years ago and 10 C.I U Clubs had been formed in Coventry since the war ended—five on sites provided by the Coventry Corporation and, no doubt, the Association had been of great help to the Officials of these Clubs.

DEPUTY POLICE CHIEF'S PRAISE

Mr Stanley Porter, the Deputy Chief Constable, spoke of his pleasure in meeting the Coventry Secretaries' Association for the first time, and looked forward to meeting them again. He had heard only praise from the Chief Constable about the Clubs. He was pleased when he was asked to deputise for the Chief, who was away on holiday

George Radburn (Branch President) presented the Lady Mayoress with a bouquet, praising her for her co-operation and for the work she was carrying out with the Lord Mayor

Pat Ansell (Chairman of the Association and National Member) then presented the Lord Mayor and Mayoress with an Old English Coventry-made Silver Tea Service. He praised the Lord Mayor for his help to the Clubs and said he knew of no person outside the Club Movement who had done more for the Clubs than the Lord Mayor

There had been a great change in Coventry's Club life during the past 15 years. They had 38 Clubs with a total of approximately 80,000 male and female members.

Great changes had been made in Club Buildings and all but one Club had carried out extensions. Eight new Clubs had been built and four old Clubs rebuilt The one Club which had no extension would be rebuilt on a new site during the next 12 months. To rebuild these 38 Clubs, with furnishings and fittings, at to-day's value would cost approximately £1,000,000. The Association paid a tribute and thanks for the co-operation of the Local Government Officials who had at all times been ready to help the Clubs.

The Lord Mayor, in reply, thanked the Clubs for their kindness. Whatever he had done for the Clubs had only been done with the co-operation of his fellow Councillors, who were entitled to the same thanks as himself

Triumphant Canley Club netball team!

For long-term Hen Lane Club member Bob Arnott, clubs were about social networking long before the term came about.

"If you wanted your car mending or someone to do some decorating, you went to the club. There was always someone offering their skills and services. Everything was there for you and you could sort it out over a few pints. It was all very convenient under one roof!"

★ **Roy Lenton:**
★ "I was a life member of the Keresley
★ Coronation and my sister had her wedding
★ reception there, marrying the steward's son!"

Coventry's clubs did seem to have it all! Some of them, however, struggled to keep up with social, economic and cultural changes in the 1970s and 1980s. A few courted controversy for failing to accept new members from all parts of Coventry's increasingly diverse communities. How they were called out for racial discrimination is part of the Coventry clubs' story.

★ **Teresa Eyden Wycherley:**
★ "In the 1970s my husband and I regularly
★ visited the clubs, dancing the night away.
★ There seemed to be a dance for every
★ night of the week with a live band. As well
★ as cheaper beer than the pubs, they often
★ provided hot food."

Coombe Social 75th Anniversary

Local band Modern Rhythm

Left: Mahinder Majhu of Hen Lane Club-the first Indian snooker referee

Cox Street Club Football XI 1950

Racial tensions and the need for unity were highlighted by Coventry's hugely popular 2 Tone music movement in the late 1970s.

Some musicians came through the discrimination to find fame and be role models to others.

Women enjoyed the clubs over many decades but could join only as "lady members" with limited rights until 2007.

Many clubs did their best to work for all their members and welcome new ones from diverse backgrounds. They adapted and survived whilst others struggled.

Other sports and social clubs were set up by Coventry's key employers: Courtaulds, GEC, Herberts, Triumph, Jaguar, Massey Ferguson and more. They all provided great recreational facilities for their employees and deserve a book of their own!

Trophy Winner at Canley Social Club

Many of clubs listed below feature in this book:

Albany Social

Amalgamated Engineers Club

Baginton British Legion Club

Barras Green Club

Bell Green WMC

Binley Miner's WMC

Brassworkers Club

Building Trades Club and Institute

Canley Social Club and Institute

Charterhouse Club

Cherrytree Sports and Social

Cheylesmore Social

Coachmakers Club

Coombe Social

Coundon Social

Coventry Colliery Sports and Social Club

Coventry Godiva British Legion

Coventry Trades Hall

Coventry Working men's club (aka Cox Street Club)

Eastern Green Social

Edgewick Trades Hall

Edgewick Social

Exhall Club

Foleshill Social Club

Foleshill Ex-Servicemen's Club

Gasworks Social Club

Coventry Godiva Club British Legion

Green Lane Ex-Services Club

Hen Lane Social Club

Howitzer RFA Old Comrades Club

Keresley Coronation Club

Lime Tree Park Social

London Road Social Club

Parkstone Club and Institute

Radford Social Club

Railwaymen's Club

Red Lane Club

Rowleys Green Working Men's Club & Institute

Royal Warwickshire Club

Ryton Social Club

Stanton WMC

Stoke Aldermoor WMC

Stoke Conservative Club

Stoke and District Ex-Servicemen's Club

Tom Mann Club

Robin Hood Club

The 1925 Club

Tile Hill Social Club

Unicorn Social Club

Walsgrave Club

West End Club

Westwood Club and Reading Room

Willenhall Social Club

Wyken WMC

So, let's step once more through the doors of some of the much-loved clubs. You might find some familiar places and faces waiting for you!

Anniversary programme 1973

COVENTRY WORKING MEN'S CLUB
54 COX STREET . COVENTRY . CV1 5PH

Souvenir Programme

**For the official opening of the new extensions
TUESDAY, 13th MARCH, 1973 at 8.00 p.m.**

By the President of The Club & Institute Union: A. Bates

COVENTRY CLUBS
SHOW HOW IT'S DONE!

CHAPTER ONE

Coventry Working Men's Club laid on a fun-filled week of events for its centenary in 1960. Over 2,000 members enjoyed the grand finale evening with 6d (that's old money!) off a pint. As the city's oldest club and one of the first in the country, there was plenty to celebrate!

Local dignitaries Lord Mayor and Lady Mayoress of Coventry, Alderman and Mrs Harry Stanley, joined the party. A clubman himself, the Mayor was "full of pride" for how clubs were run and what they did.

Coventry's Chief Constable Mr. Pendleton was also there, not because he expected any trouble - just the opposite! He thought clubs well managed and didn't cause much bother. "You have really magnificent places and I think you deserve them."

It was a group of pioneering weavers that got the ball rolling in 1860 – they wished to have their own space with a small reading room and library but no landlords or bosses telling them what to do. It was self-help among those with little money and few resources: crowdfunding long before the term was coined!

Small premises in Much Park Street were hired first before moving to New Street in 1862. It was one of the first clubs to affiliate to the Working

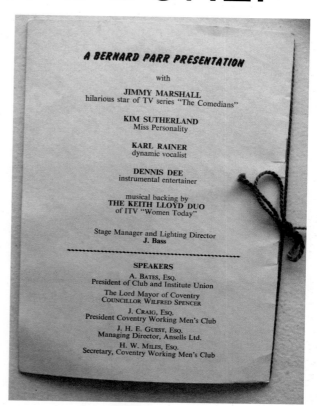

Anniversary programme

The Reverend Henry Solly, founder of the Working Men's Club and Institute Union

★ Did you know?
Temperance supporter the Reverend Henry Solly was behind the WMCIU – more often referred to as the CIU. A caring man of great insight, he believed that working men and their families would benefit from having their own recreational spaces away from pubs. His campaign to get clubs going gained the support of high-ranking people including Queen Victoria. Solly hoped clubmen would shun the 'demon drink' but accepted that it was best for clubs to decide the 'beer question' themselves.

They were ran on a private membership basis. Unlike pubs, people couldn't just walk in off the streets. Men wishing to join had to be nominated and, if accepted, paid annual subscriptions. Affiliation to the CIU brought clubs practical support and membership of a 'Union.' Local branches emerged across the country with Coventry's clubs becoming part of the new Warwickshire branch in 1917.

Men's Club and Institute Union (WMCIU) established that same year. In 1903 they relocated to bigger premises in Cox Street and that became its new unofficial name!

After the war, the club's committee saw how the city was being rebuilt around them and hatched ambitious plans of their own.

The council offered them another site but they politely turned it down.

Bert Miles was Club Secretary at the time and said: "We have always been known as the Cox Street club and we would have lost our heart if we had moved."

 Chris Mckirdy:
"My dad's favourite club was Cox Street where he was entertainment secretary and a life long member. I remember the secretary in a box who would introduce the acts and work the lights and the waiters in their white jackets taking the orders."

 Estelle Brain: "On summer Sunday evenings, mum, my sister and I used to attend Evensong at Binley Church. Dad would meet us afterwards and off to Coombe Club we would go. We'd sit outside, with a glass of stout for Mum and Vimto and crisps for us. Happy days!"

The membership of Coventry Working Men's Club reached 2,300 by 1973. The royal couple's visit in 1977 was a major triumph with Coventry's historic club emerging as one of the most modern in the city and most regal in the land!

Another of Coventry's early clubs was originally a coffee tavern but became the Earlsdon Working Men's Club in 1910. It served alcoholic drinks until losing its licence in 1931.

A member's wife - fed up with her husband's late drinking sessions - was blamed for the loss, rumours circulated that she complained to the authorities! We don't know if that's true but any club caught breaking licensing laws risked closure.

Six months later, it reopened as the Albany Club and Social Events Club. Located in the heart of a growing residential district, it soon became a popular club.

★ Did you know?
"Members of a CIU affiliated club can buy an associate pass card which opens the doors of other CIU clubs. Supporters of club teams could travel away on games nights and holiday-makers could take in the amenities of seaside clubs - CIU tourism! Pass card holders needed to be signed in by a member of the club they were visiting. These passes were not available to women until 2007."

THE WORKING MEN'S CLUB & INSTITUTE UNION LTD.

253-4 UPPER STREET

London head office

The Old Binley Working Men's Club also got on the wrong side of the law due to out of hours drinking. It opened in a small wooden hut in 1929 but was soon closed down.

The desire for a local membership club didn't disappear though so under a different management committee, a new club emerged in 1933, the Coombe Social.

The first club secretary, Mr Wallis, kept things on the straight and narrow with the club welcoming and entertaining members uninterrupted since then.

 Roy Lenton: "Sometimes went in the Cox Street Club on a Sunday night and played snooker. Also used the Builders and London Road clubs, usually for snooker."

Barras Green Club marked its 60th anniversary in 1973 with a week of special events. The founding 53 members were mostly allotment owners and started off in a shed, calling it the Chickweeds club!

They pooled their resources to get proper premises which were enlarged and improved over the next twenty years. By December 1939 they had 800 members.

Disaster struck when the club took a direct hit during the war, killing 30 people. Barmaid Lilly Green wouldn't go into the cellar before the raid, going to check on her daughter instead.

That saved her life when the club was hit.

It took the club years to recover and members were pleased to finally see a new concert hall in 1959. By the time of their 60th anniversary, the membership was 2,000 – including 100 "lady members"!

Howitzer Club- Jan Mayo's dad, grandad and uncle sitting at the back

A club with a big bang!

There was much talk of homes fit for heroes after WW1 but ex-servicemen wanted clubs to socialize in and keep alive the close bonds they had formed. They also wanted better recreational and social amenities and beer at reasonable prices.

The Royal Field Artillery Old Comrades Club opened in 1919. The founder members, who had been part of the South Midland Howitzer Regiment, bought and converted a stable in Ford Street into a club. Seven years later it moved to larger premises in King William Street.

★★★★ **Jan Mayo:** "My dad was a member of the Howitzers Club. Like many men, he was there every night of the week and Saturday and Sunday lunchtimes."

1973 saw the opening of impressive refurbished rooms with the ever-ambitious committee planning a new concert hall. Del Jones, Entertainment Secretary at the time said "There's always something happening here!"

The founders were commemorated in large murals depicting a howitzer gun and scenes of WW1 battles in France. Bert Ward and Bill Stevens, aged 84, were two early members who still used the club in the 1975.

The Howitzer had been transformed into a modern club but they still kept up old traditions such as the annual flower show, winning the CIU Warwickshire Branch Chrysanthemum trophy in 1970.

Stuart Beamish kept a small wallet for his CIU pass card permanently in the top left hand pocket of his Levi denim jacket. "Darts were in the right hand pocket. Never left home without them! No matter where you were in the country, you could pop into the local CIU club, get a drink and game of darts and have a chat."

Stuart Beamish never left home without his club card wallet!

Gary Morton was a member of Stoke and District Ex-Servicemen's Club, which was built in Clay Club in 1922. In 1960 it opened a £20,000 new hall as the club began to modernize. Former Mayor, Mr Pat Ansell, a keen club supporter, opened the new hall and praised the club's ambitious plans.

Gary Morton's Stoke Ex-Services Pass Card

The Foleshill Ex-servicemen's Club dated back to1921 when a loan of £1,200 helped secure a site on the Foleshill Road. Founder members turned it into a club and later bought the house next door to expand into.

★ **Phil Sephton:**
★ "Being from the area, my brother Dave and I would pop into the Foleshill Social and
★ other local clubs."

It wasn't until the mid-1970s that refurbishment was complete and the club fulfilled a long-held ambition. The "new look club," built around the shell of the old, had facilities and furnishings described as "second to none".

The Godiva British Legion was first established in 1922 but moved several time before finally settling until in Spon Street.
Paul Wortley's parents, George and Margaret, were steward and stewardess when the new club opened in Spon Street.
"My memories of my time at the club begin

with helping to unpack several hundred chairs to furnish the large concert room on the first floor of the building. As a ten-year-old it seemed like an adventure of sorts!"

The club consisted of a lounge/bar on the ground floor and a games room, accessed via about half a dozen steps, which housed a snooker and bagatelle table and darts board.

Paul remembers the large concert room and stage on the first floor. "I can't recall the capacity of the concert room but it appeared to be of gigantic proportions!"

He believes it cost around £67,000 to build. "A quick comparison of the value of the pound in 1969 to present would be approximately £1.1 million!"

Foleshill's Stanton WMC claimed to be Coventry's second oldest club. It instituted a roll of honour after WW1 and added to it after 1945. This took pride of place in the club. At Christmas time, the Stanton provided older members with a special dinner and entertainment.

They met at the Stanton Club! Jimmy and Flora Cooke

Alderman William Parfitt, a miner from the Rhondda, became Coventry's Lord Mayor in 1965. He sang the praises of the Stanton, declaring himself "100% for working men's clubs!"

Coventry didn't have a Wheeltappers and Shunters Club but there was the Railwaymen's Club!

Lorraine Gardner-Crofts started going to the Railwaymen's in Spon End when she was about two. "I remember when the entrance was an entry you had to go down and it had outside toilets!"

> ★ **Sue Lowe:**
> ★ There was a strong sense of camaraderie
> ★ in the Baginton British Legion Club
> ★ when I went there with my dad.
> ★ I don't think I've felt anything like it since.
> ★ The club dates back to 1929."

In Foleshill the Gas Works WMC was conveniently located right opposite the gas works. Members didn't have far to go for a refreshing pint after work!

The Amalgamated Engineers (AEU) Club celebrated 75 years in the CIU in 1986. As would be expected, there was a whole week of events with members treated to free entertainment. And some cheap beer too!

Rich Mulligan's family used the club and his dad, an entertainer, sang there.

"We had my dad's funeral 'do' at the AEU. We found a video of him singing so played it. His last gig was his own funeral where he had his first one!

It wasn't sad: it was a perfect send off. A great day, which ended with a rousing cheer for dad."

Coventry was famous for making cars so surely a Carmakers Club existed? This would be the Coachmakers Club, set up in 1918 by a group of vehicle builders at Coventry's Daimler works.

Old British Legion Godiva Club, Ford Street

A City of Cars and Coachmakers

Coventry's new Cathedral being built alongside the ruins of the old

During the blitz 1940/41, members came to appreciate the steward, Mr White, much more. The club in King Street was badly damaged but he and his wife kept going amidst all the difficulties with a cheery word and smile. He retired in 1955, after 26 years of service and was honoured at a special presentation.

The club survived the best efforts of the Luftwaffe but not the postwar town planners! It had to make way for a new ring road and moved to the Radford Road in 1958.

Coventry had several colliery clubs. Binley Colliery WMC started in 1918 with a grant of £25 to purchase a wooden hut. The club celebrated its 50th anniversary in 1969 with the opening of a new £40,000 Concert Room. The Coventry Colliery and Keresley Social Club also started small but became a popular club.

Teresa Eyden Wycherley's grandad, Tom Eyden helped to found the Parkstone Club with his eldest son Stanley.

 Mr Walrus:
"Coventry had a thriving Working Men's Club culture and a club pass card allowed entrance to all of them.
Many of them were very successful financially in times past."

"Tom was a master carpenter and he and Stan enjoyed a drink on their way home from work. They started the Parkstone specifically for people in the building trade."

The club opened in 1919 after the founders put what they could in the kitty to get things started. After two years above a shop in Elmsdale Road it moved to a building on Foleshill Road owned by a local brewery.

But this club was always on the look out for better premises. They moved just down the road in 1931. A bowling green was laid at the back and spent £4,000 on a new billiard room. Games were always high on the list of priorities for clubmen!

Tragedy occurred during the war when the club received a direct hit. Steward Vic Barrel and member Arthur Prince were killed but the club carried on.

In 1970, the club opened their new building, costing £60,000, much to the delight of the ever-growing membership.

Also in Foleshill was Edgewick Trades Hall club, opened in 1923. It famously kept its doors open during the great depression of 1926, offering what help they to those going through very hard times.

Coventry's early clubs were all unique but shared common aims and experiences as they developed and expanded!

Morgan family celebration at the Gas Club!
Courtesy of Debbie Nelson

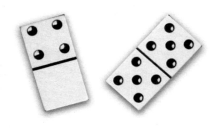

LUXURIOUS
IS THE WORD!

Canley Social Club

CHAPTER TWO ★

The war had ended but Nissen huts were still needed in Coventry - being put to good use as new clubs! Ministry of Works wooden huts were also cleverly crafted into clubs as well.

Even before the dust had settled, planning was going on at every level to rebuild war-damaged Coventry. Groups of men across the city met after work to discuss their shared goal of having clubs for themselves and their families.

As new ones were being established, older ones were embarking on ambitious expansion and modernisation programmes.

There was friendly competition to see which club could be the biggest and most luxurious!

★ Did you know?
Jimmy Cooke became Secretary of Canley Social Club in 1956, previously holding the post of Treasurer. He was a well-known clubman across Coventry and further afield. He sat on both the CIU Warwickshire Branch and National Executive committees and was a local JP for some years."

★ Margaret Cooper:
★ "My dad, Jack Smith, was one of the founder
★ members of the Canley Club. He had a
★ silver cup named after him that was played
★ for each year."

Canley Social Club and Institute's application for a club with a billiards hall and a lounge was submitted by Secretary Mr R. James in late 1948. Approved the following July, the club officially opened in 1950 and for a decade, the temporary hutting did good service.

Lynda Rowsell's dad Frank was a founder member and she remembers the old huts very well. "Dad told me they brought them over from Baginton airport and the men laid the concrete bases for them."

Mr Rowsell did a lot for the club over the decades and the local community in general benefited. "He was never on the committee but dad was eventually made Honoury Chairman of the club and also had a games shield named after him."

Christine Venning's dad Les was another founder member who rolled up his sleeves and got stuck in.

14 **Unicorn Social Club**   THE CLUB AND INSTITUTE JOURNAL   *January, 1964*

Unicorn's Lion's Share of Luxury

This might be a view of a room in one of the world's plush hotels. It is, however, the palatial new concert hall of Coventry's Unicorn W.M. Club, with the stage in the background. *Photo: Coventry Evening Telegraph.*

TIME : 1947. Scene : a member's home or public house in war-wracked Coventry. A group of men decide to form the Unicorn Working Men's Club. But these are days of austerity and money is none too easy to come by. The men—undaunted—"dream dreams" and plan ways of raising money to make them come true.

Six years later part of their dreams is realised—but only after laborious lobbying of the Ministry of Works for the building licence then necessary

During the fight for the Club's first premises—a secondhand Works Ministry timber-framed hut put up mainly by the members—the secretary then—the late Mr F J Coyle—even went to the House of Commons and enlisted the help of Mr Maurice Edelman, Coventry North's M.P

Mr. Coyle, founder member was one of the group who fought to keep the Club going from its inception. Looking back they were pleased at the time with the hut, though they dreamt of better things.

ASSETS—3s. 4d.

But the assets were only a princely 3s. 4d. However the Club developed rapidly. Funds and membership grew apace and 1956 saw the opening of the first stage of the permanent premises. This comprised a new clubroom and steward's flat, costing around £14,000.

That was Dream No. 2.

Now the third—and most ambitious—dream has come true with the opening of the last stage of the £40,000 permanent premises. It consists of a palatial concert room to seat 300, TV lounge, committee room and ancillary accommodation, plus a bar with 40ft. long counter.

Planning started in 1960 and the work was completed five weeks ahead of schedule. Membership now stands at about 800.

In the concert room, whose ceiling is lined with natural polished timbers, with contemporary style decor several thousand pounds have been spent on furniture and fittings and an electronic organ has been installed, costing £1,000.

POLICE CHIEF'S HIGH PRAISE

It was in the concert room before a number of distinguished visitors that the "dream" building was officially opened by Mr. Baillon. The Chief Constable of Coventry, Mr. E. W. Pendleton, warmly congratulated the Club on the "wonderful" standard of its premises and took the opportunity of expressing unequivocal praise of the good management and conduct of all the C.I.U. Clubs in Coventry.

At the same ceremony Union Executive representative Pat Ansell presented Club Life Membership certificates to Vice-President B. Hill, Secretary E. Johnson and Treasurer L. Laxon. With President W Steane they each received an inscribed tankard.

Mr. Hill is the only one of the original members still in office.

To Steward W. Dixon, Mr. Ansell presented the Club's gift of a silver cigarette case with a silver bracelet to Mrs. Dixon.

Among those present were Alderman H. B. W Cresswell, who as Lord Mayor opened the Club originally, and Councillor Bob Loosley. They were asked by speakers to convey to the Corporation thanks for advice and wonderful assistance not only to the Unicorn Club but to other C.I.U. Clubs for which they had earmarked sites in the redevelopment plan.

From Warwickshire Branch were President H. Shaw and Secretary J Stringer, and the ceremony was followed by a variety concert, during which a large celebration cake made by a member, Mrs. Evans, was cut and enjoyed by the many people present.

CHRISTMAS CHEER FOR O.A.P.s

THANKS to the generosity of Cwm Clubs Skittles and Darts League, the village's old-age pensioners had a brighter Christmas.

The proceeds of the League's annual knockout competition (£57) were presented to the Cwm O.A.P Branch at the Comrades Club when Mr. S. Weeks (O.A.P Treasurer) said it was hoped to give a present of 15s. to each aged couple in the area. About £160 was needed to do this.

"Your contributions are the life blood of the organisation," he said, "and without people like you we could not exist."

Thanking all who had taken part in the League he mentioned that in the past three years he had received a total of £170 from them and he was pleased the players spared a thought for the old folk.

The League has existed more than 30 years and has helped the old folk for many years, handing over to them an average of £50 per year.

CLUBS ADMITTED TO MEMBERSHIP OF THE UNION

Stanley Irish Literary Institute, Station Road, Stanley, Co. Durham.

Cwmsyfiog and District Ex-Servicemen's, 54 Queen's Road, New Tredegar, Mon.

CLUBS APPLYING FOR MEMBERSHIP OF THE UNION

Phoenix Bowling Working Men's, Charleston Street, Ashton Road, Oldham, Lancs.

Cockenzie and Port Seton Branch British Legion Social, West Harbour Road, Cockenzie, Prestonpans, East Lothian.

City Engineers Department Sports and Social, New Central Depot, Foleshill Road, Coventry, Warwicks.

Ashby Labour, Bottesford Road, Ashby, Scunthorpe, Lincs.

Carnforth and District Ex-Servicemen's, Scotland Road, Carnforth, Lancs.

Blackhouse Workmen's, Beech Ville, Edmondsley, Co. Durham.

Cheam Social, 111 Church Hill Road, Cheam, Surrey

CLUB CEASING MEMBERSHIP OF THE UNION

Tamworth Road Social (Derbyshire Branch)—closed.

Children's Christmas Party in
the old Canley Club hutting

"He helped to dig the foundations. The club was always of paramount importance to him, right through his life. After he died, we found his membership cards for every year since it opened - they were really carefully wrapped up."

Expansion involved a new games room, lounge and bar and then a new concert room and beer cellar in 1963, with the club rapidly becoming one of the biggest in town.

Canley made the last payment on the mortgage to the city council in November 1967- not bad going! A celebratory event was held and club President, Mr Jack Bailey, thanked all the members.

By the early 1970s a new bar, impressive games room and lounge had been built with more refurbs in the pipeline. There were plenty of celebrations - each time something was completed there'd be glasses raised!

The Unicorn's founding members in 1947 shared the dream of many others to have their own social club. But they had a few battles about the building

licence and enlisted the help local MP, the Right Hon Mr Maurice Edelman.

Six years later the dream became a reality and another name was added to the growing list of Coventry's clubs.

At least three Coventry clubs made use of Nissen huts: Bell Green WMC, Lime Tree Park and Green Lane Ex-Servicemen's.

Lime Tree Park Club was set up by ex-fireguards during August 1947 in two converted Nissen huts. Mr. Harold Dunn was a founder member and first club president. The club quickly grew so it had to move.

The Midlands Clubs Brewery loaned them £6,000 to build the first proper premises. By 1954, a new bar, lounge and billiards room had been added and finally a concert room, opened early 1962.

★ Did you know?

A club was established once the official paperwork was all done. It didn't need to have a building: that could take years. That's why the year a club was established and when it officially opened aren't always the same! John Reynolds said that it used to be 'much easier' to set up and run a club. They simply had to send five shillings and a list of 25 members to the Customs and Excise office and 'that was it!'"

Happy
winner at
Canley!

Coventry City Centre in the 1950s

Left: Lady Godiva statue- a gift to Coventry from William Bassett-Green

Club supporter MP Maurice Edelman was happy to pull the first pint in the new bar. "Everyone in Coventry should be proud and I hope this club will long be an example to the CIU. Only the best is now good enough for the working people of this country. You have really set a pattern to the rest of Britain."

Green Lane Ex-Services Club was set up in two Nissen shelters used for carrying out tank repairs during the war. A group of local ex-service men raised funds to buy them then transformed them into a social club for local people.

They were fortunate to be given the land by William Bassett- Green, who funded the iconic Lady Godiva statue. A local treasure for Coventry people, it came to symbolise the post-war regeneration of the city.

Bell Green Club, opened in 1956, later moved to bigger premises in Rosebury Avenue. Its location on an expanding housing estate meant it quickly attracted members and was extended as numbers grew in the early 1970s.

Tile Hill Social skipped the temporary building phase, being a purpose built club opening in 1962. It took years to get planning agreed though the land had been allocated by the council after the war.

> ★ **Did you know?**
> *"The late John Reynolds was noted for his club work - and signature moustache! He was the CIU's Warwickshire Branch President for many years and a National Executive member. He first went to the Charterhouse Club in the 1930s with his founder member father and enjoyed the Christmas parties. He went on to be help establish Tile Hill Social and became its president. Not only club-going but club building ran in the family!"*

> ★ **Chris Mckirdy:** "Our families have been involved in Working Men's Clubs all our lives. My dad was the secretary of Bell Green club when it was in Deedmore Road."

One name proposed was Westwood Labour Club but Tile Hill Social was chosen, in line with other clubs named after the estates where they were built.

By 1971 it had "state of the art" upper floor premises. Further extensions and refurbishments came in the 1970s, making it one of the largest clubs in Coventry. The concert hall had one of the biggest stages in the West Midlands and by 1981 it had around 1,500 members.

They even planned a swimming pool! That would

The Lord Mayor of Coventry, Alderman Harry Stanley, himself an enthusiastic Clubman, triumphantly holds aloft the first pint he has just drawn to officially open the fine new games room at London Road Social Club, Coventry. He handed the pint to B. Mohan, for 11 years Secretary and a member of 33 years' standing. Left to right in this "Coventry Standard" photo: B. Mohan (Secretary), E. W. C. Pendleton (Chief Constable), Alderman Stanley, President C. Woodhead, Steward A. H. Robinson, Warwickshire Branch President G. Radburn and Mrs. Robinson (Steward's wife).

The first pint in London Road Club's new games room!

really have made a big splash but along with plans for a cycling track, didn't happen.

Friday 13th January 1967 was lucky for Foleshill Social Club! After completing a major modernization and extension programme, the new lounge with "luxurious" furniture was opened. The old concert room had been turned into a games room.

Kaga Simpson recalls the treasure hunts by car run by the Foleshill Social. "We'd be given clues then drove out, one clue led to another till the final destination."

Willenhall Club played host to many CIU dignitaries and events over the year but it had its own royal claim to fame. The club welcomed Princess Margaret in 1982 when she was on the official duty of inaugurating a nearby church.

John Reynolds remembered her well. "She drank Famous Grouse Whisky and had a gold cigarette case. She would rummage around in her handbag, bring out the cigarette case and then ask 'does anyone have a light?'" Plenty of men did!

 Tricia Pearson:
"My husband was a member of the Radford Club and I met my future in-laws at the Coronation Club in Keresley."

Female harmony group Sweet Feelings topped the bill for the Radford Club's 75th anniversary in 1994. Comedy duo the Burns Bros provided some laughs for members in the packed concert room. The club had come a long way since it began in a house in 1919!

The "Eight Great Gentlemen" founders met regularly in local pub the Grapes to discuss their plans and each put in £25. Quite a sum back then! Others soon joined them and within a few days they had over £700. Its early popularity brought a move to bigger premises with a billiard room and later a concert room built in the late 1930s.

Walsgrave WMC also began very small at the centre of the village in the early 1920s. Newly refurbished in 1976, it was another Coventry club referred to as one of the "most luxurious" of its kind in the Midlands.

Only a few years later the club's popularity brought further extension. "We have 1,900 members now and a waiting list that's likely to get longer as housing development continues in area," Dave Davies, Club Secretary said at the time.

That's how the club remained till 1975 when its membership stood at over 2,000 with a long waiting list. A major modernization project then gave the club a new £70,000 a "plush super room."

Situated close to a cemetery but full of life, that was the London Road Club. It had to relocate from it home of 40 years due to redevelopment in the late 1950s.

CANLEY CELEBRATES 25 YEARS' PROGRESS

The National President with the Canley committee.

25 years for Canley Social!

, Branch EC member Bart Hart, Branch president Harry Shaw, club treasurer Sid Rawlings, club president Jack Bailey, Derek , club vice-president Eddie Cullan, Jim Cooke, Branch secretary Jack Stringer and Branch vice-president E. Hartopp.

The new club boasted facilities for darts, dominoes and two full-size snooker tables. Alderman Harry Stanley, Lord Mayor and active clubman, officially opened London Road's new games room in September 1957 and, as tradition demanded, pulled the first pint!

He told those there that the city's working men's clubs were equivalent to any gentlemen's club and the local authority liked the way the clubs were developing.

1,000-seat concert hall will be the pride of Coventry's biggest club

WHEN rebuilding is completed Willenhall Social Club will have spent £120,000.

FROM a one-room bar eight years ago to the biggest club in Coventry today—and a challenging determination to be the biggest club in the Midlands before very long.

That is the record of Willenhall Social Club, which this year is undertaking alterations to the tune of £45,000.

When the alterations are completed in 1965, the Club will have a 1,000-seat concert hall complete with orchestra pit, dressing rooms and kitchen.

An electric organ costing 1,600 guineas will rise from the orchestra pit when required.

"By the time the concert hall project is completed," says Mr. Tommy Ferguson, founder-president, "the Club will have spent over £120,000 on buildings."

2,000 MEMBERS

The 40 founder members of 1956 have increased to a present membership of 2,000 and the committee had to close the membership list six months ago. Willenhall is part of a cosmopolitan area of England, so it is not surprising that the Club membership includes Poles, Italians, Greeks and Hungarians in addition to English, Irish, Scots and Welsh.

Two factors account for this record expansion. A general committee and officers who are heart and soul in the Club, giving every minute they can spare and determined that every amenity within the range of Club life shall be available to their members.

Many of the committee of 18 are founder members. Ray Atkinson and his wife Beryl are the full-time Steward and Stewardess. Ray is a founder member, as is secretary Jack Chambers (full time since 1961).

BIG CENTRE

Secondly, the Club has set such a record for entertaining that it is the

sportsmen in many fields. Boxing is popular (the new hall will be used for tournaments). Eighteen amateurs train at the Club. There are two football teams. The angling section has 40 members. Snooker billiards, darts, dominoes and crib are also popular. But tombola beats the lot—seven sessions a week.

Three times a week professional artistes are engaged by the entertainments com-

mittee, and after the bingo sessions free-and-easy concerts are held.

Willenhall members have every reason to be proud of their achievement. It is an outstanding example of the qualities that have made Clubs such a virile and successful part of the national life. It is a safe prediction that the committee won't stop with the present extensions programme but will soon be looking for new fields to conquer.

And good health!
● "And may we long see you on the other side of the bar," Mr. Alan Loveday receives a cheque on his retirement after five years as assistant steward of the Whitefriars Press Club, Tonbridge, Kent.

£500 aid for blind Clubmen

Willenhall Social undergoing transformation

Celebrating Jimmy Cooke's 40 years of service

And the ladies received bunches of flowers!
Warwickshire CIU event

As a child in the late-1940s Tricia Pearson looked forward to Sunday nights when her family went to the 1925 Club in Freehold Street. "As I got older I went to other clubs - the Spencer Club in Albany Road and the Wyken Club."

Wyken WMC unveiled their new "concert room on stilts" in 1963. The stilts were concrete pillars under which was a member's car park. Before pulling the first pint, there was praise from Coventry's police chief Mr Pendelton. "You have got the very best and you deserve the very best!"

When the club began in 1935 in two miner's cottages, founder members had a £10 whip round to fund it.

★ **Liz Smith:** "My dad played snooker at
★ the Wyken Working Men's club. When new
★ premises were built in the mid-1970s, it
★ was one of most modern clubs in the city."

Mr George Winterburn became club secretary and helped set up the popular Wyken WMC male voice choir.

John Schofield remembers a very important day in 1987 at the Wyken WMC - that's where he and his friends watched the Cup Final in which Coventry City FC emerged triumphant!

February 1964 brought an important occasion for Hen Lane Social Club when it opened an extended and refurbished concert room. Mr. W. Pruitt, Club President said: "This is a day we have been looking forward to for a long time."

You'd think that Hen Lane Club would be in Hen Lane but it's in Beacon Road. In its early days, it was known as the "little Rhondda club" with its establishment largely the result of the efforts some Welsh miners who moved to Coventry for work. Opened in 1936, the club always had a strong Welsh feel, complete with a male choir.

Hen Lane grew in popularity so nearby land was brought for expansion. The new room was seen to have "every modern facility" and able to seat 500 people. There was also a car park for members that became so busy in the 1960s and early '70s that the club employed a part time attendant!

Coventry's clubs, old and new, all added more than a touch of luxury for their members to enjoy!

Having a drinks with pals at the Lime Tree club

Hen Lane Club group of friends

46-YEAR-OLD GRANDAD BEATS STEVE DAVIS
- ONLY IN COVENTRY'S CLUBLAND!

Hen Lane Club Cups Cabinet

CHAPTER THREE ★

Maybe it was the fact that snooker was one of the most popular games in Coventry's clubs that the players were so good at it.

But few could have bet on a 46-year-old grandad beating world champion Steve Davis. But this is exactly what happened when Lime Tree Club snooker-mad Tom James played the man himself who was visiting the club in 1985.

Daughter Jayne Ramsay says: "Everyone knew my dad, he played in the snooker team at the Lime Tree Club." It made a big splash in the local media: "46 year old grandad beats Steve Davis!"

Jayne's dad considered turning professional as a young man but there wasn't the money in it then. Her mum jokingly called herself a "snooker widow", as did many women, but the family were extremely proud of their champion.

When Jayne's dad passed away the Lime Tree snooker team had a wreath specially made in the shape of a snooker table. This moving tribute showed the close bonds and team spirit that formed between club players.

Games were the lifeblood of the clubs in their heyday. For some men, and women, they were actually more important than the beer! Many club members took part for the fun and sociability, others because they were in it to win it!

They were following in the footsteps of parents and grandparents as the games go back to the

Young Steve Davis setting out for snooker success!

19th century clubs when billiards was popular. This game of skill was played in the gentlemen's clubs that many early WMCs aspired to.

Something else to be proud about was that the Coventry games league became the largest in the country!

When Willenhall Social hosted the Coventry and District CIU League's Annual Cup presentations in 1970, over 250 representatives from almost every Coventry club were present!

Sports trophy Canley Club

Prizegiving at Canley Social

There were scores of activities, or sections as they're called. Hen Lane Club was known across the country for its hospitality when hosting the national championships for cribbage, a very traditional club game.

Radford Social, on the other hand, was the first in the country to establish a golf section and the CIU added it to their long list of recreational activities.

 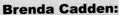

★ **Brenda Cadden:**
★ "I remember the games room at the
★ Canley Club and the men playing
  bagatelle. There were all age groups
★ playing the games, young and old,
   having fun and enjoying it all until
   time was called."

A keen lot of golfers, 107, showed up at the Grange Golf Club when Radford Social organised their Second Annual Golf Tournament in 1972. Tee-off was at 7am and it lasted till dusk.

Brian Moffitt of Stoke Ex-Servicemen's Club eventually lifted the CIU trophy to become the new champion.

The Radford Club has always taken the games seriously. When they opened a new billiards hall in the late 1930s, they had no fewer than eight tables, which attracted more members.

Coombe Social Trophy Cabinet

To get away from it all, some men joined the angling section.

David Withers was a keen member of Tile Hill Social's Angling Section in the 1970s.

"Great memories waiting for the coach at 6am Sunday morning. It was always full. Happy days! I fished for Tile Hill and also Lime Tree club, 1973 to 1979."

Canley Social's Angling Section enjoyed a long weekend in Ireland in 1966. A cine-film of the trip was made from the time the happy anglers left the club to their return. This was shown at the Annual Dinner and Trophies Presentation, held at Canley Social.

CIU Recreational Secretary Mr Gen Ding was there to open the club's "amazing" new games room and said he'd rarely seen such an array of trophies and prizes. "Coventry Clubs have set a high standard and Canley has once again demonstrated what can be done."

Coventry WMC opened their new games room "with a difference" in 1972. It not only had a carpeted floor but a special aircon system and was thought to be the only Coventry club with such "refinements."

Walk into any club and the trophy cabinet usually has pride of place. Full of shiny cups and medals won by teams and individual players, it highlights the central role the games played in club life.

These were not just idle pastimes but games of skill, some taking years to master. That was particularly true of bagatelle, a table and cue game. Related to billiards, it definitely required

Coombe Social games room

A great achievement for Mahinder!

Pete Potter was a fan of Lime Tree Club's snooker tables when he was a motor vehicle student at Tile Hill College.

"Wednesday was our full-day at college. Dinner times were spent at nearby Lime Tree Club where we played on the superb snooker tables they had there. What a great club it was!"

They also downed four pints. "We fell asleep at our desks within five minutes of being back at college. The lecturer teaching vehicle electrics hadn't got a chance with his image of a battery, a switch and a bulb to explain a simple circuit!"

Snooker ace Steve Davis dominated the game during the 1980s, reaching the World Championship eight times and winning it six. He was also snooker's first millionaire!

Like other successful players, Steve never forgot that his career began in CIU clubs. When he visited Coventry clubs for exhibition games fans

Left: You have to concentrate! David Reith, Canley Social Bagatelle player

patience and Coventry clubmen excelled at it.

Young men would stand by and watch in awe as older members played bagatelle. The seniors could often be seen teaching younger ones how to play this and other games. They were good mentors, passing skills and advice to the next generation.

Linda Anne Wolohan's dad, James Kelly, used to be the captain of Tile Hill Social's bagatelle team.

"He reached the Coventry Individual Bagatelle final but was beaten by Bell Green Club's Bill Sympson. We were very proud of him!"

Football not snooker had first brought James to Coventry. "He transferred to Coventry City FC from Dunfermline FC in 1957 for £10 a week!"

Long before snooker was televised, clubs were the places to watch players with skills that now enthrall millions.

And Coventry can be proud to have the first Indian man to become a certified snooker referee - Mahinder Majhu. Hen Lane Club member Sandy is rightly proud of his father who passed all the exams to gain that accolade in 1990.

"Everyone knew my dad as Fred. He organised matches across the country. He was the first Indian gentleman to become a professional snooker referee."

The first Indian snooker referee Mahinder "Fred" Majhu

Inset: Mahinder Majhu's Snooker Referee's badge

Tile Hill Social Bagatelle team

On the ball: Tile Hill's Pete Clusker eyes up a bagatelle shot during a Coventry CIU Games League match. Looking on, left to right, are: Ralph Lapworth, Peter McGovern, Jeff Inesson, John Taylor, Alan Crilly and Jim Kelly

would pile in to see him, hoping to learn something of how he worked his magic!

Helen Reith once had the pleasure of serving him with a batch at the Canley Club! She was helping out her mum who ran the food hatch at that time.

When Steve visited the Parkstone Club in 1983, he made quite an entrance on a brewery's dray complete with horses and a drayman walking alongside.

 Simon Russell:
"Dad played for Foleshill Social darts team. The darts tournament always ended up back at ours for drinks. Great days!"

Another snooker champ, Joe Davis (no relation) visited Coventry clubs including Radford Social in the 1950s and '60s, to show his professional snooker skills.

Darts is another traditional game that pulled in the crowds. Coventry clubs brought in some of the big players (no pun intended!) to play exhibition matches that thrilled members.

Scottish darts ace Jockey Wilson was one of them. He appeared at Willenhall Social in 1982, the year he won the World Professional Darts Championship.

Rob Summerfield remembers the darts legend John Lowe doing an exhibition at the Stoke Aldermoor Club. "My Dad played him but John won!

Games nights saw coachloads of players and supporters travelling across the city. The home club members liked to get in early, as there would be queues of visitors showing their CIU pass cards and getting signed in.

There would usually be some food laid on, another reason to get in quick. The Hen

Lane Committee resolved in November 1965 that: "hot batches be given to the players on games night." Most clubs offered cheese and biscuits, sandwiches, chips and cocktail sausages.

Boxing

The Victorian thinking was that if young men are going to fight, let them do so with rules. The boxing tradition established by early clubs continued well into the 20th century.

Sheila Bates' uncle Robert William James had his nose broken in a street fight so took up boxing, later becoming a trainer at Stoke Ex-Servicemen's Club. During the war he served in Italy and the Americans took him on to train their boxers. That's when he met the great Joe Louis!

Sheila's husband also had some boxing lessons at the Stoke Ex-Services. He met Sheila's uncle there and was surprised to meet him again on their wedding day!

Sheila Bates says "I think my husband took up boxing, as young men did in those days, and represented the youth team at Cox Street WMC."

Mark Rewhorn's dad boxed at Edgewick Trades Hall. "The room above the bar was a gym and you could often hear the thumps and bumps that come from training and sparring. I remember pictures around the room of successful boxers that they had trained - my dad was amongst them!"

European and Commonwealth medal winner Danny McAlinden - or "dangerous Dan" as he was nicknamed - boxed at the Edgewick Club. He was sometimes spotted running round the local park as part of his training programme.

Willenhall Social was also big on boxing and had a new hall built in the 1960s for training sessions and matches.

What about football?

Barry Savage lived opposite the Canley Social as a lad, which had a field but no pitch.

"Frank Rowsell was a founder member and he supported this idea of having a football team. They ploughed the field to make the pitch. We kids all helped with buckets to collect bricks and other

> ★ **John D'Arcy:**
> ★ "Tile Hill Social was known for its very
> ★ successful amateur boxing club. Their
> ★ coach was the much-respected Billy Duffin.
> ★ They even had an ABA finalist around
>   1975, the very talented James Cooke."

debris from the field. Our reward was a bottle of pop and bag of crisps!"

They held regular club matches as well as making the pitch available for other teams. In 1961 the club successfully applied to have a football pavilion built. For many years it was a great sporting facility for the whole community.

Keith Hicks joined the Coombe Social on his 18th birthday in 1962 and helped lay out a football pitch for the club team on nearby common land. "The team was quite good in their day but had no pitch of their own. Later on they had a pitch at the back of the club, until that was then sold."

No ladies on the tables!

Even though the games room was often seen as a male preserve, women and children could go in, but usually to watch the menfolk play. Not for women the joys of chalking up the snooker cue.

Meryl Barrett's sums up a typical experience for women.

"The Albany Club was the only place I was taken for a night out by my first husband and it involved watching him play snooker. Not a great night out

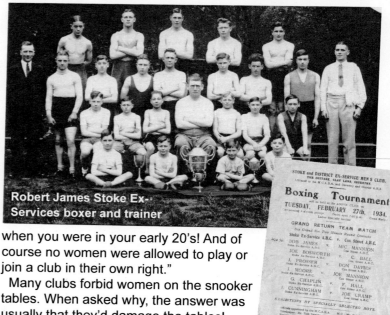

Robert James Stoke Ex-Services boxer and trainer

when you were in your early 20's! And of course no women were allowed to play or join a club in their own right."

Many clubs forbid women on the snooker tables. When asked why, the answer was usually that they'd damage the tables!

But whilst for many decades there were no female snooker champs, you could certainly find them at the darts board.

Super Gran and the first woman sportsman of the year!

The Radford Social's ladies darts team was very proud of long-standing chair and ace player Irene Lawson. Team mates called her "super gran", as she played for Radford for over 50 years, well into her late-eighties.

Irene took up competitive darts by accident in the 1950s when she stepped in to help out a friend's team at the Howitzer Club. They won the game! No surprise they wanted her in the team after that. Irene went on to win many prizes, local and national fame and was a founder of the Coventry CIU Ladies darts league.

Canley Social football team

Radford Social's Ladies darts team

Nostalgia
A LOOK BACK AT THE SPORTS TEAMS OF YESTERYEAR

EVERYONE loves reliving their glory days on the sports field and remembering the characters and clashes of years gone by. The Telegraph shares your old team pictures every Saturday.

Irene's girls still throwing strong

COVENTRY-BORN Irene Lawson, of Bulwer Road, Radford, sent in these pictures of her ladies' darts team at Radford Social Club.

Radford's Winning Women Darts Team

On retirement she became its honorary president.
As women participated more in games and sports, there were more women's sections and leagues, including netball. Judith Peters' skills and achievements in the Canley Club netball team brought her a great accolade.

"I am proud to say I was the first female to be voted the Canley Club's Sportsman of the Year!"

Marion Hughes was another keen member of Canley's netball team. "We were very successful in our time. We came third in the top Coventry league to the likes of Henley College and the GEC. I played from 14 to 33 years of age, just loved it!"

Not having a netball court didn't deter Canley's keen ladies. "We started off playing on the car park, before they built the court," Marion recalls. "We probably played there for about three years from when I started, around 1973/4."

Their determination paid off as they gained their own court and many successes.

Bowls was popular with both for men and women. In 1970 the Bell Green Club Bowls Section annual presentation welcomed around 100 guests. The section, founded in 1963, had one of the youngest bowlers in the country, 14 year-old David Burdett.

Another first for Coventry's clubs!

Roland Davies would sometimes go with his father to bowls matches. "The Monday night's games teams went round different clubs. On various occasions I did the bowling scores cards with my father."

There were plenty of games and sports to keep club members busy and the benefits included an active social life and long-lasting friendships.

Canley netballing team champions 1979

Canley Social's netballing team receives awards

Canley Social's successful netball players

Dominoes!

ALL YEAR ROUND **FUN** FOR ALL THE FAMILY

CHAPTER FOUR

Canley Social Children's Christmas Party

With sports days, Easter bonnet parades, beauty and Glamorous Grandmother competitions, there was never a dull moment at Coventry's clubs! They pulled out all the stops to offer year-round activities for all the family.

Looking after the kids!

The children's Christmas parties were a big highlight of the year and the mums helped with the food and refreshments. No child went home without a present, a belly full of pop and trifle plus lots of good memories!

Jan Mayo remembers how much kids looked forward to the Howitzer Club's parties. "Such exciting times for us!" Norma Stephens remembers the Christmas stockings given out.

Kate Hart's memories of the Wyken Working Men's Club parties include her providing some of the entertainment!

"There always used to be a gap in the proceedings and kids were invited up to perform. I'd play my recorder and Stylophone, even getting paid in two pence pieces. I remember them shouting 'where's the girl with the recorder!' I'd run home to get a whole assortment of them. Must have been hellish for everyone!"

Just to have a night out at a club with their parents was excitement enough for some children.

For Chris Mckirdy it was a big outing on a Saturday night. "We came from Bell Green and my dad and I would get two buses to go the Coundon Club."

Tricia Pearson's family went to the 1925 Working Men's Club and in pre-bingo times, Sunday was concert night.

"There was usually a singer and a comedian. The children sat at the front and we had a packet of crisps, usually Robinsons, with Coventry's three spires on the front on the packet, or Smiths, and a bottle of pop."

Mum's work is never done! Children's Party time at Canley

As kids in the 1940s and 1950s, Jan Mayo and her brothers and sister were taken to the Howitzers Club, usually Saturday nights and in the summer holidays.

"We loved it! We would watch dad play bagatelle and sometimes move the arrow along on the scoreboard for him. My younger brother Geoff would be lifted onto one of the tables and he would sing his little heart out, to everyone's delight."

★ **Chris Mckirdy:** "One time my friend and I went up on the stage at the Cox Street Club. We had to sing and the person gave us half a crown and told us we were now professionals."

Jan also remembers that occasionally they would have a film show upstairs. "I remember seeing one called The Glass Mountain."

Children would be sat outside on the lawn at the Radford Club with the obligatory bottle of pop and bag of crisps. There was an informal keeping an eye on kids by mothers, who would take it in turns to check on them. Children would have to behave or they'd get their father in trouble with the committee!

★ **John D'Arcy:**
"Tile Hill Social was a great little club where youngsters met up with their friends and parents discussed how their children were turning their hair grey over a few drinks and many laughs."

Rich Mulligan's debut as a musical child prodigy didn't go too well. His dad was a club singer and Rich got "dragged round all the clubs". One time his dad got him to play trumpet. "The fact that I couldn't play seemed of little interest to him till I totally humiliated myself and him!"

On the plus side, he did go to a lot of club Christmas parties.

But children were not always welcome and there were complaints!

Hen Lane Lunchtime get-together

The Hen Lane committee considered "the question of the behaviour of children in the club" in April 1965. The majority voted that children would still be allowed on Saturday evenings but had to behave themselves.

★ **Christine Venning:**
"The Canley Club was so important for my dad, especially after mum died in the mid-80s. He went twice a day after he retired for the company and continued until the day before he died."

Phil Bunn remembers being on his best behaviour at that very club. "I would sit next my dad, my ankles together with a glass of pop and a bag of crisps, not moving much. Behaving myself!"

Michelle Poyner Conroy's main memory of the Canley Social is of summer play time activities with afternoon film shows and talent competitions. "The late Doreen Godson was the playtime leader. Brings back happy memories to think of those times!"

Roland Davies ran a disco for the kids on Canley Club's big field for the Queens Silver Jubilee celebrations in 1977.

An unpleasant part of the club experience for children was the smoky atmosphere with as so many people constantly had a cigarette on the go. Jan Mayo remembers this at the Howitzer Club.

"It was like a fog. I used to have to go out into the alleyway at the side of the original club

Summer time fun for Canley Social kids!

Entertaining the kids! Canley Social

because of the smoke from all the cigarettes. By the end of the night my eyes would be streaming."

Older members had their own special activities and events. Free beer was often included!

The local Holbrooks OAP Association was granted the use of Hen Lane Club's concert room in the 1960s.

The Canley Social Club threw their annual Christmas concert for their OAPs in late November 1978. The "jovial pensioners had a night to remember". The pensioners committee ran weekly raffles to raise funds for the events, always a popular part of the club's calendar. This was what most clubs did across the city.

> ★ **Wayne Millward:**
> ★ "My childhood years were spent going to
> ★ the Canley Social Club. Christmas parties
> for the kids were fantastic. It wasn't perfect,
> ★ nothing is, but it seemed people were
> ★ more together then."

In 1972, Coventry WMC ran Tuesday morning sessions for their older members. They met in the games room to have two free pints of beer with sandwiches and to enjoy any game they liked to play. Sometimes the lounge was opened and the senior members, including former entertainers, put on a "first-class" variety show.

Over 200 Canley senior citizens were entertained at the club's annual Christmas dinner in December 1977.

Each member received £1, gift tickets and sat down to a "super" meal. Afterwards the ladies had cigarettes and a glass of sherry while the men received cigars and a glass of whisky, plus £3. There was a show band for entertainment.

At the AEU Club's annual dinner for OAPs in 1976, 90 year-old Fred Brougham received a special welcome. He was number one on the membership list meaning he was the oldest. Fred and 149 other participants enjoyed "an

exceptionally good dinner" and a variety show.

Rick Hough thought that for widowed men, such as his grandad, trips to the club were a lifeline.

"It got him out of the house and into company. The twice-daily visits to the Canley Club broke up the long days of monotony and loneliness that old age can convey. He'd have a few friendly words with the barman and some of the regulars. If his friends were in, he'd engage in some light mickey-taking! There was always a genuine affection and interest in each other's families and the daily struggles of life."

Rick's time spent with his grandad at the club brought some bonding over a few pints. Rick also learned more about his grandad's war-time experiences. "He knew that he had been involved in something momentous but I don't think he ever really valued the magnitude of what he'd done. After all, many of his peers had similar experiences."

What about Women?

Wives and daughters of club members increasingly participated in club life in the postwar era, finding their own space for relaxation and leisure.

But there remained some spaces out of bounds! Roy Lenton remembers that before he was old enough to go in the bar at the Coronation Club women weren't allowed in.

At the Radford Social, it was the late 1950s when

> ★ **Brenda Cadden:**
> ★ "I used to love going to the Canley Club,
> the people there, the hustle and bustle,
> ★ the laughs and the jokes.

members were invited to bring their wives to the club on an "unrestricted basis"!

A group of women at the AEU Club formed their own "section" and organised their own entertainment. They held a social event every

Family night out at the Hen Lane club

A night out and natter with friends

Tuesday and ran it themselves. They said it gave the committee, all men, a night off! They had their own space for a few laughs such as fancy dress parties and concerts.

The Willenhall Club offered friendship and social life for Trev Teasdel's mother after his dad left. "Going to the club really helped her through that bad time, the club worked for her in so many ways. It was a kind of social support system, people helped each other in hard times and had a knees up on the dance floor!"

Bring on the dancing queens, beauty queens and glamorous grannies!

The popularity of beauty competitions may have raised eyebrows among feminists but they attracted big audiences in the 1970s.

Girls night out at the Club

Tile Hill Club held the CIU's Warwickshire Branch's Queen of Clubs competition in June 1970, with the large concert room "packed to capacity." The Unicorn Club held their first beauty contest for "ladies between 16 years and 18 years of age" in the same year.

Steve Cooke talks of them as being "a sign of the times" back then though probably frowned upon today.

"Nobody was forced to take part! There was no modelling career guaranteed from winning although some national winners did go on to Miss England and Miss Great Britain."

Some women wanted to try their luck on the club stages. The competitions were a "bit of a laugh" and offered glitz and glamour, even if just for a night.

Steve Cooke knew a bit about the competitions as he attended many from an early age with

A Knees-Up down the Royal Warwickshire Club

his parents. Jimmy Cooke was Secretary of the Canley Club and along with his wife Flora were often asked to judge at the regional competitions.

"Queen of Clubs was a big deal back then. The winners from each club went on to the Coventry and Warwickshire competition and then to the national competition held in Blackpool's Winter Gardens."

"Any local bias was taken into account somehow!" As a family they often attended the final in Blackpool. "That was tough for a 15 year old adolescent I can assure you!"

> ★ **Sylvia Weller:**
> ★ "What fun we had in those days. The Canley Club was always full and we had so
> ★ many things going on."

Ballroom dancing was another activity supported by many clubs. In 1970 the Warwickshire Branch held both its Ballroom Dancing and Queen of Clubs competitions at the Tile Hill Social with the large concert room "packed to capacity." Mrs Margaret Wilson of Tile Hill Social beat 19 other entrants to win the Queen of Clubs title.

In 1971, the Queen of Clubs and Modern Ballroom Dancing competitions were held at Willenhall Social. Mrs Rose Hurst of Canley Social Club won the beauty contest with Les and Barbara Mace of Stanton Club triumphing on the dance-floor.

Helen Reith entered the Canley Club's Queen of Clubs competition in 1977. "I entered under duress! Well, not really. My friends Maggie and Brenda talked me into along with them. On the actual night they backed out. And I won!"

Helen's beauty queen career came to an abrupt end at the next round. "We had a coach trip from the club for the next competition but I came home defeated."

Helen still has the sash she was presented with on her victory. "My Nan Lillian Pinker actually

made it! I can't bear to ever part with it."

A Canley Club woman triumphed the next year at the Warwickshire Queen of Clubs! The £150 first prize and a place at the national finals in Blackpool went to Jane Brooks who only entered as a bit of a joke.

"This will be my first and last beauty contest. Once I've been in the national finals, that will be it!"

Jane already had a busy life teaching PE at Binley Park School and playing in Canley Social's netball team.

It wasn't just younger women lining up on club stages. Willenhall Club hosted the first finals of the CIU's Warwickshire branch Glamorous Grandmother competition in 1970. The winner was Canley Social's Mrs Martha Villiers.

Tile Hill Social once again hosted the Glamorous Granny and Old Time Dancing competitions in 1972 plus the Queen of Clubs. Mrs Verona Sampson from the Canley Club won the Glamorous Grandmother title.

Joe Lee, a former Canley Social steward, remembers these competitions well. "The glamorous wife of our insurance man who lived up the road from the club went on to win the national competition."

These contest certainly challenged people's typical views of grannies!

Adults only!

A form of club entertainment that wasn't for all the family was the striptease shows popular in the 1970s. The "swinging sixties" had helped to bring about some loosening up in terms of what was acceptable on stage. And that in included some loosening of clothes.

Canley Social Queen of Clubs line up 1977

Left: Looks very serious! Junior Beauty Queen Contest Final

Easter Bonnet winner Mrs Joan Woodcock

Top: Helen Reith crowned Queen of Canley Club! and the Queen of Clubs winner's sash

Changes in regard to stage nudity meant performers could move around as they casually discarded their clothes. Sunday lunchtime strippers shows were staged after which the men headed home to their roast dinner.

Radford Social was known to have performances by Sheba. Her clothes were carried off by her very tidy daughter!

Women were not left out as male strippers also started strutting their stuff on stages across the city. They could be booked for hen nights, birthday or just to bring in the crowds and a bit of income for the clubs.

Wedding bells and Easter bonnets!

Apart from each club's annual events, members hired rooms to celebrate family occasions such as birthdays and wedding receptions.

Carol Stafford had her wedding reception at the Tile Hill Social in 1970. "It was great community amenity where families could have get-togethers including the kids. In those days pubs weren't

very welcoming to kids, most wouldn't let them in. Clubs did."

Tony Roscoe also had his wedding reception in the same club, in 1994. His verdict? "It was a great!"

★ **Margaret Cooper:**
★ "We were the first to have a wedding
★ reception in Canley Social Club's brand
★ new posh concert hall in 1964!"

Easter time brought not just chocolate eggs but another popular event on the club calendar – the Easter bonnet competition! A number of clubs in the area held parades and various competitions around the holiday period.

Mrs Joan Woodcock was a keen participant in the Canley Club's, making the winning bonnets several times in the 1970s.

From the very young to the very old, whatever the occasion, Coventry's clubs did their best to look after everyone.

Best place for a birthday bash! Games room Canley Social

Wedding Reception Party

ALL ABOARD THE 'CHARA'!

CHAPTER FIVE

Howitzer Club Men's "Chara" and beers!

Coventry is a long way from the seaside, whichever direction you go in. Before cheap package holidays, the club's summer outing was the only time some children, and adults, saw the sea. It meant the world to them. The trips would usually take place during the Coventry holiday fortnight when all the factories closed down.

 Nick Edgington:
"My grandad worked the door at a local club for years. I remember we had a few chara trips to Blackpool, with crates of brown ale for the chaps and pop and crisps for the kids. Don't know what the ladies had!"

So eagerly anticipated was the Howitzer trip that Jan Mayo could scarcely contain herself. "I was so excited waiting for the coach outside the club that I wet my pants and left a little puddle on the floor!" Jan was probably not the only child to have a little accident.

The early clubs set down the tradition of running excursions for members and an early means of transport was the charabanc - an open topped carriage with wooden benches. Cheap and cheerful, but not exactly comfortable! No wonder crates of beer were needed to ease the journey. The committeemen assigned to oversee the trips probably needed some refreshment too!

Motorized, covered versions came into use in the 20th century. Long after charabancs were replaced by coaches, club trips were still often referred to as "going on a chara!"

Estelle Brain remembers Binley WMC organising seaside outings to Barry Island, New Brighton and Skegness. As they were a club set up by local

miners, they also ran coaches to the Miners Gala Days, held each year in Tamworth.

"Loved the seaside trips, especially the visit to Barry Island, my dad's brother and family lived there. On arrival the children were all given a bag of sweets and strips of free tickets for rides in the fair. Packets of crisps and bottles of pop were distributed on the journey!"

Hen Lane Club's dedicated Children's Outing Committee decided on New Brighton for the 1964. Another trip was to local attraction of Alton Towers. The club record books states: "Children's outing- a vote of thanks was recorded to the Committee for their successful efforts re. the children's outing to Alton Towers."

Robert Waggitt's earliest recollections of the Albany Social are of the children's outings. "We used to go to Wicksteed Park. All the children were given a coloured badge to wear that got you into the canteen for your dinner at a certain time. I think we also were given some money to spend during the day."

 Tricia Pearson: "My friend Jan's dad used to get me a ticket from the Howitzers Club for their children's summer outing, usually to Skegness or Wicksteed Park."

Wicksteed Park, in Northamptonshire, was opened in 1921 by philanthropist Charles Wicksteed. His "people's park" featured a large lake and a railway which was always popular with children, some adults too!

As children Norma Stephens and her siblings were taken to the Lime Tree Club and went on their trips to Wicksteed Park.

On the day of Radford Social's club trip, five or

Jan Mayo loved the Howitzer Club Children's Outing!

Canley Club Committee Men's Outing

six coaches would be lined up all down Beake Avenue bright and early. Eager travellers would be milling around with their picnic hampers and macs. People who weren't going would come to wave them all off! This would be the typical scene outside any club the day of the excursion.

Right: Club Outings to other clubs!

Another popular destination was Dudley Zoo, first opened to the public in 1937. Apart from the zoo, with its modernist buildings, the grounds included an 11th century castle and limestone caverns. Plenty of opportunities for kids to have adventures and give their parents the slip!

It was not unknown for clubs to hire whole trains for day trips or longer excursions! Radford Social was one that took some members on holiday by train.

John D'Arcy recalls to Tile Hill Social organising an annual seven-day trip at the September break to Blue Waters Holiday Camp in Seaton, Devon.

Some trips were very local indeed but nonetheless keenly looked forward to, especially to the annual pantomime.

Estelle Brain felt from her own experience that her local clubs, Binley WMC and Coombe Social, really looked after families. "Apart from Christmas parties there were visits to the pantomime at the

Hippodrome for the children. Two or more coaches left the club for the Saturday matinee. At the Hippodrome we were given bars of Fry's Creme chocolate!"

Not all the club outings were for the children: the men made sure they had their own!

Not surprisingly these would call in at other clubs and pubs and crates of beer would be loaded onto the coach for the journey.

Trips were also organized to breweries such as Burton-upon-Trent, which at one time brewed around a quarter of all the beer in England!

Going continental!

In 1972, some members of the AEU Club's Ladies Section took the club trip up a level or two! No coach or train for them- they flew off to "the Continent" as Europe used to be called then for a "memorable" weekend!

The ladies took a chartered flight from Baginton airport to Amsterdam where they "made the most of the nightlife!"

Made a change from Skeggie!

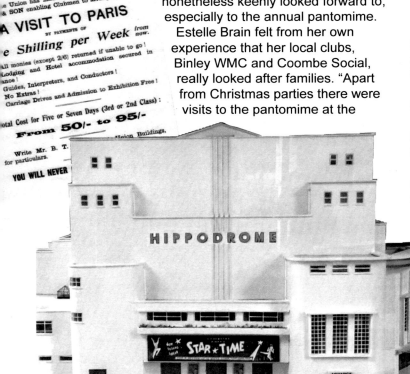

The place of Panto heaven! Model of the Coventry Hippodrome

COVENTRY'S **PALLADIUM** AND TOP CLASS ACTS!

CHAPTER SIX

Sing-a-long at the Howitzer!

"It's all happening at Hen Lane Social," ran the Clubland headline in the Coventry Evening Telegraph, February 22nd 1978.

The club was staging its first "spectacular" for St. David's Day in the new-look concert room with a "nightclub atmosphere." Top of the bill Welsh comedienne Stella King had some Max Boyce numbers lined up in her act.

No surprise about the Welsh theme! Hen Lane's was called the "little Rhondda" club in its early years. Entertainment Secretary Dai Williams, whose father was one of founder members, said: "We thought this would be a good opportunity to officially christen the new-style room."

 Simon Russell: "I still have fond memories of the Friday night 'free 'n' easies' at the Foleshill Social with the stage bedazzled in glitter. Think Phoenix Nights only with everyone I grew up with! All the old boys would get up to sing. It was a fantastic family night out!"

In a previous refurbishment of the concert room in 1964, the new "top class" stage microphone was identical to the one at the London Palladium! At the touch of a switch it rose from the stage to any height.

During the 1960s and 1970s Coventry's clubs were undergoing extensive modernization programmes. The Willenhall Social opened

a 1,000-seat concert hall for its 2000 strong membership in 1965. Described as the "pride of Coventry" it had an orchestra pit, dressing rooms and a kitchen. The electric organ, which cost 1,600 guineas, could rise from the orchestra pit.

Photo shows some of the members of the Coventry WMC enjoying one of their social gatherings.

OLD clubmen in Coventry not only enjoy the facilities of the clubs but actually take part in entertaining themselves. The Coventry WMC has a session every Tuesday morning when they meet in the games room, have two free pints of beer with sandwiches and enjoy any game they like to play. Sometimes the lounge is opened. It is then the turn of senior members who put on a first-class variety show.

At the height of their careers as entertainers they were prominent in Midland clubs, with names like Val Mack singing songs from the shows; Jack Cotterall, who was a well-known tenor and is still in good form; Leo Burns, comedian and violinist who at one time played with the Coventry Hippodrome orchestra under the leadership of Charles Shadwell; Frank Lovello, clown who although he is over 65 is still in great demand at children's parties and holiday camps. Doing excellent service at the piano is usually Albert Statham, who has accompanied many artistes over the years.

In the summer, somewhere around 200 members from Coventry WMC go on a

day's outing with money in their pockets to spend.

The Stanton WMC is another club which provides for older members with a feast at Christmas.

In the summer they also go out into the country to enjoy themselves.

The Edgwick Trades Hall club give their members a monthly grant. At Christmas the amount is much larger to cover their special seasonal requirements. The income for this purpose is raised by a weekly tote and an occasional raffle.

Coventry WMC Entertainment

Joe Reynolds on Sax with Modern Rhythm

**Above:
Local
band
Modern
Rhythm**

Member's expectations were also on the rise, so every club "ent sec" was on the look out for top class acts. But sometimes a traditional 'free 'n' easy' went down well, with members taking to the stage to sing or tell a joke or two.

★ **Alan West:**
★ "The Zodiacs played every second Sunday at the London Road Social Club back in the
★ 1970s/1980s. Top band!"

Frank Rowsell often played the piano at Canley Social for a good old sing-along. Daughter Lynda says: "The poor thing was partly deaf and he would sometimes lose the tune half way through, so did a 'twiddly bit' on the ivories!"

After a few pints, the members probably hardly noticed!

★ **Jan Mayo:** "My late husband played lots
★ of the working men's clubs in the 1960s
★ and 1970s. He was the drummer in a group
★ called the Countdowns. They played mostly
★ Shadows music but could manage any of the
★ popular dance tunes."

For Joe Reynolds the 'free 'n' easy' was "the thinking man's precursor to karaoke!" The quality varied: mixed in with talented members were those who really should have stayed sat down!

On Rich Mulligan's list of songs that were "regularly slaughtered" in the 'free 'n' easies' are: Ten Guitars by Engelbert Humperdinck, Paper Roses, Isn't She Lovely and Fly Me to the Moon!

Liz Smith reckons Delilah was top of the Free 'n' Easy charts whilst for Sue Long it was Hi Ho Silver Lining.

At the Canley Social Joan Woodcock was noted for her rendition of What a Difference a Day Makes and Nicola Crane's dad sang Blueberry Hill.

The resident musicians, often drummer and organist, accompanied paid acts and 'free 'n' easies'. These guys didn't exactly have job

security though. The Hen Lane club committee in November 1965 "moved and carried that the drummer be dispensed with".

Mark Drewitt thought Tile Hill Social was "a brilliant place for friendship and entertainment" and resident organist was his best mate Ray Freeman.

Local talent

Many popular acts were local people making a bit of extra money on the club circuit. Happy to perform at weekends as light-relief from their day jobs their acts might even have been their alter egos! There were a few who became full-time professionals and some made it into the "big time."

Johnny Mac and the Collectors played many of the clubs in the 1950s through to the 1970s, including Keresley Coronation Club and Wyken Club.

Bob Brolly and Calvary were firm local favourites along with Smackee. Meryll Barrett saw both groups at Tile Hill Social and Canley Club. "I remember thinking how good they both were."

Christmas 1978 was a busy time for Smackee who had just returned from a cabaret engagement in Dubai. They were booked for Parkstone WMC, Coventry Colliery Sports and Social and Coventry WMC.

★ **John D'Arcy:**
★ "There was always an 'act' on Saturday
★ nights at Tile Hill Social. They also had a
★ resident MC, Colin Scott. He was a really
★ good singer and also a founder member of
★ 1970s pop group New City Sounds."

Calvary was also very busy over the Christmas period. For local musician Lee Ross, "Calvary was definitely at their height back when our band - Take Five - were getting started, early 1980s. I think they had secured the M&B contract. They were regulars at Stoke Ex-servicemen's, Willenhall Social and Coundon Club."

Local Entertainer Lee Ross

The Zodiacs were regulars at the Stanton, Walsgrave WMC, London Road, Cox Street, Willenhall Social and the Lime Tree clubs. Coventry music historian Pete Chambers describes them as "one of the hardest working bands in the areas, one of the first few rock and roll bands in the city."

They appeared on TV's talent show New Faces in September 1977 and performed Last Night we Called It A Day. Everything didn't go right on the night so they didn't do as well as they perhaps deserved.

The Barry James Trio was another busy local outfit with Jim Tallentire on bass, son Derek on lead guitar and son Barry on drums. Sister-in-law Pamela was guest vocalist and bass player.

Godiva British Legion concert

Jim's father was an organist and bass player so music was clearly in the family's DNA. The band won a talent contest in 1966, coming first out of 92 entrants. They played across Coventry and Midlands and were very popular at the Canley Social as some of them lived very nearby.

★ **Lee Ross:** "In the early 1980s you had to get set up and sound checked not long after 6pm as people would be queuing to get in way before 7pm. Our first spot was often 8pm or even before. Unheard of these days when no-one goes out till at least 9-10pm! The holy grail for us at the time was to get regular work via the brewery, like Calvary or Smackee secured, where you were guaranteed bookings four or five nights a week or even a residency."

With so many clubs and talent across the city, the ents secs formed an influential network. It was hard to impress these men if you were a wannabe club performer!

18 year-old Lee Ross definitely thought so. "I asked myself, what have I let myself in for?" Lee's band was going into their first "shop window," where they could show what they had to offer.

They knew Bill Maltby, Ent Sec at Canley Social, was going to be there. To get the nod from him meant that you were in. Lee makes a comparison with Simon Cowell today!

Radford Club Anniversary Programme

The Zodiacs was another popular band, formed in the 1950s after musicians Maurice Redhead and Nigel Lomas met at Coventry's Drumbeat Club. Other band members included Graham Peace and Terry Wyatt.

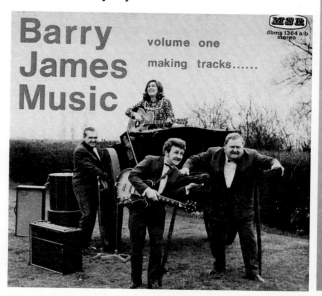

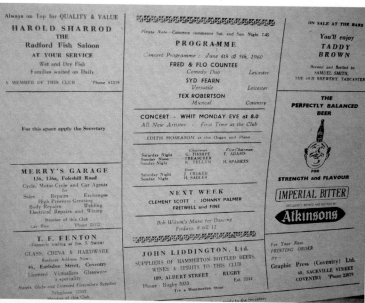

Margaret Cooper's dad Jack Smith at Canley Social

Bob Monkhouse, comedian and TV presnter

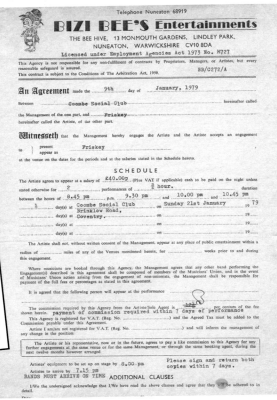

Friskey Coombe Social Contract

Lee's band did get the nod. "Bill Maltby was very strict but very good at what he did. He'd be there at the club door to meet you, shake your hand, would do the full job."

Canley Club opened their £50,000 "new look" concert room in 1978 and the 3000 members were keen to use it as much as possible.

Local musician Joe Reynolds spent a lot of time playing in cover bands including Modern Rhythm between 1982-84.

"We went through a number of line ups which included Lieutenant Pigeon's Nigel Fletcher on drums, Clive Cook

New City Sounds flyer

28 Arnold Avenue
Styvechale
Coventry

FRANK DEMPSEY (Manager)

★★★ NEW CITY SOUNDS

Telephone : Coventry 411846

AKA Paul Chase, and Delsy Griffiths AKA Ruby Washington on vocals."

At the Spencer Club one night, drummer Nigel's friend Don Powell from Slade came to sit with the band's wives and girlfriends.

"A lovely bloke, very friendly. The Birdie Dance was part of our set. Don pulled my wife up onto the dance floor and proceeded to do the dance with all the right moves while we played it!"

New City Sounds had various line-ups over the years, after forming in 1969 at the West End Club. Sadly, tragedy struck early on when Mick Hayes was electrocuted on stage and sadly died. Band

NEW CITY SOUNDS
OPPORTUNITY KNOCKS
WINNERS THREE TIMES
Number One in the I.P. Polls

LIEUTENANT PIGEON

Flight of Fancy

14 Evening Telegraph, Thursday, November 13, 1986

The Entertainers by Chris Arnot

Ploughing on in face of despair

FOR Coventry showgroup Flight of Fancy it was a night of despair.

It was their first gig for their new agent. And very nearly their last.

Four of them set off by car for a working men's club in Corby. Their equipment had gone on ahead in a van driven by road manager Dave Reddington, with bass player Ray Begg in the passenger seat.

Ray thought Dave knew where they were going. Dave assumed that Ray did.

Result: the van covered most of the highways and byways of that busted Northamptonshire steel town while the rest of the band paced around the club in rising panic.

They were due on stage at 8 pm. By 8.15 there was still no sign of speakers, electric keyboards or drum kit.

When they finally arrived, they set up in 10 minutes flat (it usually takes an hour and a half).

On the way to the bar for a much-needed interval drink, they were stopped in their tracks by a thunderous clatter. Completely unprovoked, the hastily-assembled stack of bass speakers had toppled on to the keyboard, scattering like so many broken teeth before plunging off the stage.

The audience were too engrossed in bingo to notice. The caller's voice hardly faltered. Eyes remained firmly down.

It was the sort of experience

Donna Elkington: a veteran at 23

that could easily have broken the spirit of a group who were only formed in May this year.

But Flight of Fancy are made of sterner stuff. They played on through the second half with keyboard player Cherry Rudge banging a tambourine.

The keyboard's back now. Cherry was playing it to good effect on Sunday night at the group's regular venue — the Plough on Coventry's London

Road — though I noticed she'd set it up well away from the speakers which were piled precariously on top of beer crates.

At the far end of the bar, landlord George Avent stood with a poppy in the lapel of his sober grey suit, a pipe dangling from his mouth and a stray piece of hair flopping across his forehead.

He looked as though he might be more at home at a recital by the Warwickshire Symphony Orchestra.

The lounge bar regulars at the Plough are predominantly male. Rugby club badges and broken noses are much in evidence. They might tap their feet a bit to a long-forgotten Mary Wells number, but they rarely put their hands

together — not when there's a pint in one and a cigarette in the other.

Clad in a coat that finished just below her trouser bottoms and dangly earrings that seemed to finish just short of both, singer Donna Elkington put everything into it.

Her gutsy Tina Turner impression came straight from the soul. But the applause was noticeable by its absence.

If this bothers Donna, she's not one to show it. At 23 she's already a veteran. She first sang *The Way We Were* at the Town and Country Festival at the age of 13.

By the time she was 16, she and big sister Sharron were fronting a six band called Electro Motive Force (or EMF) at a time when the

music coming out of Coventry was making the rest of the pop world sit up.

In all this she was encouraged by her father, a club singer who went under the name of Don Earl and whose bath-time renditions of Mario Lanza were apparently powerful enough to stop people in the streets of Longford.

Encouragement was not so forthcoming at the home of lead guitarist Bob Drury.

Flight of Fancy: Donna (centre) surrounded by (from left) drummer Phil Vickers, keyboard player Cherry Rudge, bass player Ray Begg and lead guitarist Bob Drury.

Understandably perhaps, his father didn't take kindly to the amplified racket coming from his offspring's bedroom.

But as the lad learned to play the guitar and use it to good effect in a succession of groups, Mr Drury Senior developed a growing appreciation of rock music. Now in his late 50s he is, according to Bob, "into Meatloaf".

He's also into Flight of Fancy. "Everything to do

with the band... [text cut off] "him," says B... amused and p...

He's a fath... with an 11-ye... called Cloo an... as sales mana... products firm.

"I've got to... o'clock tomo... he remarked o... val on Sunday...

But at least... he was going...

---

members nearly called it a day but agreed that he'd want them to carry on.

And carry on they certainly did! Not only did they play most of Coventry's clubs and build up a large fan base, but went on to appear on, and win, Opportunity Knocks- twice!

When Pete Chambers asked band member Arthur Griffiths about the Opportunity Knocks experience he replied: "It was absolutely brilliant!" They had a triumphant return to the Parkstone Club and were treated like stars - probably because they were! "We packed the place out, it was sensational."

Everyone wanted to talk to them and their "as seen on TV" status ensured they packed out concert rooms for a long to come.

Bob Drury ran several bands over the years, including Friskey and Stax that played the clubs. Joe Reynolds remembers seeing his Flight of Fancy at the Coundon WMC.

The big names!

Joanne Sweeney frequented Tile Hill Club. "It was always fun at the weekend when entertainment was on and lots of big names passed through the place over the years."

Pam Parker recalls seeing the Searchers there

Look no further! The Searchers are here

about 25 years ago! John D'Arcy also saw the Searchers at Coventry WMC in the mid-1970s.

"I was about 16 and went with family and friends to see a 1960s revival show. There were a fair few acts on. One was The Searchers who sang Needles and Pins among a few others, and Billy J. Kramer, who had a hit with Little Children."

Drummer Eric Delaney closed the show and was his favourite act. "Superb foot-stomping drumming, fit as a fiddle."

Willenhall Social had a great track record for entertainment and booked some top acts such as Del Shannon.

Guitarist Bert Weedon was a Coventry favourite and played at the Radford Social in 1969. The club, with a membership of 2,200, was celebrating their 50th anniversary with a week of special events. Leicester band the Dallas Boys also appeared.

Dating back to the 1950s, the Dallas Boys were described as Britain's first boy band and were regular faces on TV, as well as at Coventry's clubs.

All the way from Leicester- the Dallas Boys!

Flight of Fancy article

DALLAS BOYS

THE GRADE ORGANISATION,
REGENT STREET,
LONDON, W.1.

You're having a laugh!

Tony Unwin generally "wasn't really a WMC sort of person".

But when he ventured into the Walsgrave WMC one evening in 1980, he ended up in stitches.

"It was a night featuring two comedians: Mike Reid (top of the bill) and Paul Melba. Paul Melba was hilarious and totally stole the show. Mike Reid was somewhat subdued as he obviously realised he had been upstaged. Afterwards my girlfriend and I went backstage to get some autographs. Paul Melba was great."

Comedian Larry Grayson loved to work Coventry's club stages - they were home territory to him. Born William White in 1929, Larry was brought up by adoptive sister Flo in Nuneaton, a few miles north of Coventry.

He went straight into the comedy scene after leaving school at 14, supporting a drag act with the stage name Billy Breen. He later changed it to Larry Grayson.

His act was rather risqué, with references to "friends" such as Everard, Slack Alice and postman Pop-it-in-Pete. These were made-up characters but loosely based on people he had come across. Audiences never tired of hearing his catchphrase- "shut that door!'"

Larry toured the UK for over 30 years, mostly drag, variety shows and the clubs before becoming a TV star in the 1970s. He once quipped that it took him 40 years to become an "overnight'" success.

Larry's favourite clubs included Cox Street and Radford Social. Biographer Mike Malyon wrote: "The ents sec at Cox Street, Wal Jones, knew he had a guaranteed full house when Billy (Larry) occupied the popular Sunday lunchtime slot."

Bobby Joyce remembers seeing the young Nolan Sisters, Krankies and Charlie Williams at Canley Club. "I literally wet my pants laughing at Charlie Williams, bless him!"

Comedian Charlie Williams

Husband and wife comedy duo The Krankies were not locals - Ian and Janette Tough (Wee Jimmy) were famously known for being more Scottish than Scottish! But they lived in the Finham area of Coventry during the 1980s. Perhaps the local vibe helped them to career success first through cabaret, clubs then pantos and TV.

Other comedians that appeared on Coventry club stages include Frank Carson and Chubby Brown.

Club members had to be careful when a comedian

Almost local lad Larry Grayson!

was performing to avoid becoming part of the act! This happened to Mark Rewhorn's wife in the early 1980s.

"We were at the Coombe Social, always good for a night out. We'd booked to see a comedian. Arriving a bit late, we ended up at the front of the concert room by the stage - never a good idea with a comedy night!"

When Mark's wife got up to go to the toilet in the middle of the act, the comedian seized his chance.

"My wife was slim and dressed in a white outfit with knee-length brown boots, He described her as looking like a 'bl**dy dipstick'. The room was in an uproar and for a long time."

At the interval the comedian bought a round of drinks for them, thanking Mark's wife for being "a good sport!"

When muscle man Tony Holland won Opportunity Knocks in 1964 for flexing his biceps, buttocks and more, he started a new craze. For a while muscle men were all over the clubs, all tight trunks and oiled bodies! Other oiled bodies came in the form of fire-eaters! Health and Safety regulations not so strict then as now.

Chris Mckirdy was taken to Cox Street Club as a child. She would sit patiently at the front to see the acts, clutching her autograph book. "They would always start with a man or woman singing opera or really old songs that made me cringe. It was so boring! I was waiting for the final act, usually a group or magician."

The magicians Mark Rewhorn saw as a child at Edgewick Trades Hall Club started his interest in how their tricks worked.

It was all magic, of course, to experience this wonderful array of entertainment on offer the clubs in their heyday!

FEELING LUCKY?
TOMBOLA, TOTES & BANDITS

CHAPTER SEVEN

"Eyes down, look in!"

When Trev Teasdel's mum went for a job interview at the dole office in 1977, they asked her what her hobby was. Her reply? Bingo!

"They laughed but she explained how it had been a big help to her during a hard time. And she got the job!"

Bingo - love it or hate it- had become central to club life by the 1970s. Whenever there was the chance of a prize or bit of cash, Coventry's club goers were keen to be in it to win it!

Within five minutes of entering their club members would be buying bingo and raffle tickets or having a go on the "one armed bandit", as slot machines were called.

Hard to believe that in the 1960s running games of tombola or housey-housey as bingo used to be called, could have got a club committee into serious trouble with the law!

They had to keep up with constantly changing gaming and gambling laws to ensure club members could continue to play this popular game. There was a bit of trial and error in the 1960s about what was allowed but rules became clearer.

Bingo was not to be run for private gain - any

money raised was to go to the club or a designated charity. Limits were set to the prize money. Likewise with the "bandits", limitations were set that changed over the years.

★ **Chris Mckirdy:** "I remember that when bingo was on at the Coundon Club all us children would be eagerly waiting outside for the 'man in the van' to come. He would be selling bags of sweets and giving out fruit. The bingo was boring and you had to be quiet."

Clubs have always had to raise money to fund their costs, amenities and activities and games of chance had proven to be effective. In the early 20th century whist drives were popular. Members paid a small fee to play and had the chance of winning something, whilst the club raised some funds.

The building of Coventry's newest club, the Cheylesmore Social, was facilitated by bingo! The club opened in 1972, but planning had begun in the late 1950s. A group of people keen to have a club in the area met regularly to find ways of raising sufficient funds to build one.

Bingo sessions began in 1961 with 20% of the proceeds going towards activities for older people and children's party funds. Work on the Quinton site began in 1971 and Cheylesmore club opened in February 1972. It affiliated to CIU later that year and very quickly had almost 900 members.

Clearly a club was needed in that part of town. Members could enjoy playing bingo in the concert room which held over 400 people and visitors from other clubs came along too.

Snowballs and Sunday lunchtime bingo!

There were two types of snowballs in clubs - neither had anything to do with snow! One was a popular drink for ladies and the other a game of bingo that paid out more. The tickets might cost a little more but the prize money would be worth it, if you won of course!

There was often a catch, such as the "full house" having to be called under a certain amount of numbers. If that didn't happen, the game carried on with the usual amount paid when the house was called. The snowball prize money would be played for the following week with more added to it. Hence, the snowball - what now would be called a rollover.

Hen Lane Club committee decided in January 1964 that tombola was to be played on Friday evenings with a snowball, two houses and a bumper house be run when the existing snowball was finished. A few years earlier the committee

resolved that "a prize of 40 cigarettes be given for the draw on the tombola."

Some clubs linked up with others and amalgamated the prize money. These special "link" games attracted big crowds. Alarm bells rang for some in the Government with fears of housewives spending all their housekeeping and neglecting the kids!

> ★ **Paul Wortley:**
> "Bingo was on a level with religion I think. I once accidently blew a light bulb at the Godiva British Legion Club and caused a power outage. It stopped the entertainment for a while. My saving grace was that it wasn't a bingo night otherwise I fear I would have been hunted down by the bingo players and beaten to within an inch of my life with bingo pens for interrupting the game!"

Most clubs ran "flyers" which were set tickets where more money would be paid out. As with the snowballs, these would usually be played near the end of the bingo session so people would stay on for the big money and perhaps spend a bit more on drinks.

Mr Walrus remembers going to the Parkstone in the 1970s and 1980s.

Bingo time!

"The bingo prizes ran into hundreds while the mid-session house prize ran to a thousands pounds or more."

Limits were eventually set to snowballs and other bingo games with higher payouts.

Bingo was taken very seriously by the players, caller and the checkers, as well as the Government!

Woe betide anyone who made any noise while the numbers were being called. An expectant, tense hush came down with stifled sounds of swearing when people were "sweating on one".

Some audience participation was permitted, such as whistling when "legs eleven" was called or shouting "clickety click" for 66. Number ten always got a response, which varied according to who was Prime Minister, "Maggie's Den" being one of the polite ones! There was also some ribbing of the caller as long as it didn't go beyond the unspoken rules.

> ★ **Mark Rewhorn:** "Sunday lunchtime bingo
> ★ at Coombe Social. Any time a woman called,
> ★ there was a grumble around the room, 'get
> home and cook the bloody dinner, woman.'
> ★ Thatcher was in No.10 and any time that
> number was called all you could hear was,
> 'get her out!'"

"Shake 'em up!" was another permitted audience cry which dates back to the times before electronic bingo machines when the caller had a small bag with the numbers in which he'd shake up every now and then.

Talking too loudly could get you into trouble. Even the bar staff were sometimes told off for washing glasses while bingo was being played.

And it was very bad form to call a "bogey"! You might be laughed or booed at for interrupting the game. Those who called too late –you had to shout as soon as your winning number was called– or on the wrong number couldn't continue playing on that ticket.

Hen Lane, as with other clubs, developed clear rules early on. The committee minutes of March 24th 1957 noted:

"Any player making a false call shall have his or her ticket destroyed after a check has been made." Making a false call was a "misdemeanor".

Another thing to avoid was winning a flyer or snowball if you were a visitor at another club. Locals might see you as robbing them of "their" money!

If a committee member or their wife called, that didn't go down too well either, as Mark Rewhorn discovered one Sunday lunchtime at Coombe Social. "The biggest laugh of the session was when one of the committee called and won the flyer. He simply stood up and shouted, 'cease!'"

Stuart Beamish played football and darts for the Coronation Club and darts for the Shepherd and Shepherdess Pub. The captain was on the Coronation Club committee.

"One night he was calling the bingo, someone called the line, so they did the checks, all ok. They should then have carried on with the rest of the card, but Gerry pulled the lever and dropped all the balls back in! Uproar! I thought he was going to be lynched!"

A women's game?

Bingo was certainly popular with women, a game of chance they were allowed to play. Men played as well, and over the years in increasing numbers as it was a way of winning some money when short time working and unemployment began to bite. It also provided a bit of social life for older men.

If a woman called a line or a full house during a Sunday lunchtime session, there might be calls for them to "get the dinner on." What might now appear to be very non-PC was a bit of bingo banter and women gave back as good as they got! Those multi-tasking women playing would probably have already put the Sunday roast in the oven anyway!

Tile Hill Social ran bingo several times at week with Thursday being the "big money" night, as John D'Arcy recalls. "The flyer house regularly paid out well over a hundred pounds. Quite a sizeable sum back then".

His mum was lucky enough to win it once. "This was really good timing as the following Saturday we were going on a week's holiday!"

For some women, playing bingo with friends was their social life and they looked forward to going to their own club and others across the city.

Trev Teasdel's mother was one of these.

"Playing bingo helped to get her through a tough time after dad left, to build a social life. And a monthly win at bingo often paid an essential bill!"

Below: Private gain

Clubs—Self Government by All

THE Lord Mayor of Coventry, Alderman Mrs. Emily Allen, J.P., opened the extended concert room of Hen Lane Social Club on 8th February.

Mrs. Allen said: "Working Men's Clubs are examples of self government by all. You organise your own Clubs, elect your own officers. It is an example of self government similar to local councils where we represent you."

The Lord Mayor and the Lady Mayoress, Councillor Mrs. Elsie Jones, were presented with inscribed silver spoons by Mr. W Pruitt, Club Secretary.

He said: "This is a day we have been looking forward to for a long time."

The room now has every modern facility and seats about 500 people. The stage is 26ft. wide and 25ft. deep, and all lighting arrangements are controlled from a compact rostrum.

The stage microphone is identical to the one at the London Palladium. At the touch of a switch it rises from below the stage to any required height.

The extended concert room, costing some £18,000, and earlier the provision of an extensive car park, are only the start of the Committee's plans. Extensions of the present bar and foyer to the concert room, a new Secretary's office and committee room, a library and restaurant are also planned. There will also be a restyled entrance to the Club.

ACCENT ON FAMILY LIFE

Speakers at the opening included Messrs. E. McEnery C.M.D. (Union President), G. F Ding (Education and Recreation Secretary) and E. W Ansell (National Executive). They all highly praised the far-sightedness of the Club Committee and the members' support.

Mr. Bob Pattison (Club Secretary said: "We have no fruit machines. We encourage family life in this Club."

During the evening Mrs. J Pruitt (Club President's wife) presented a cheque for £10 to Mr. D T R. Gray (Appeals Secretary Kent Branch Women's Convalescent Home).

Gaming machines and 'private gain'

CLUBS are earnestly reminded that the nett proceeds of such machines MUST be devoted to the purposes of the Club. Any arrangement whereby the owners of the machine —possibly a company renting it to the Club—shared part of the nett profit or benefited from the nett proceeds, would be a breach of the provisions of the law relating to "Private Gain."

The Union Executive, therefore, recommends that Club Committees PURCHASE outright Gaming Machines if they feel they must have such machines in the Club.

Alternatively they can enter into a bona fide Hire Purchase agreement, or rent machines. But they should take care that you do not enter into any H.P. or rental agreement provides for the Company (or individuals) with which the agreement is made, to have any share of the profits from the machine.

Grange's Lighter Fuel Record

LIGHTER fuel box collections at Grange Home in 1963 were at £160 16s. 10d. a record and Superintendent R. Pendrill Convalescent Homes Secretary Bill Daul trey and the Union Homes Committee say a very warm "thank you" to all who contributed to this magnificent total.

It is heartening that the Residents have shown in this practical manner their appreciation of the comfort and service provided at the Home.

Amounts collected by months: Up to March 26th—16s. 10d., April—£13 3s. 0d May—£12 16s. 8d., June £18 6s. 11d July—£14 16s. 1d., August—£25 16s. 2d September £28 1s. 4d., October £19 1s. 5d., November—£15 3s. 8d., an December—£3 4s. 4d.

Running "Housey Housey"

Below: Old Bandits!

The local vicar criticised her for frequenting the club when money was tight but in Trev's view "it really helped her out."

Don't stop the bingo!

When the Radford Social Club were building a £70,000 "super room" in 1975, members had to go without a concert room for several months. That may tough but the results were viewed as well worth it with the new room like a plush nightclub, described as "one of the best in the Midlands."

Bingo carried on regardless during the works, being played instead in the games room after two of the five snooker tables were temporarily moved out. Can't imagine that went down too well with the snooker players!

Did bingo kill club life? Some members thought that was the case by the 1970s.

Teresa Eyden Wycherley was one of them. She and her husband used to enjoy the cabarets and dancing in Coventry clubs but bingo changed all that.

"The decline started when bingo was introduced in the interval. People would arrive at the start of the evening just to get their seats. They talked and walked around all the way through the music spoiling it for those who had come for the cabaret.

Eventually the clubs realised it was cheaper just to have the bingo all evening and the bands died out. Dreadful shame!"

Roy Lenton also thought that clubs were becoming too bingo-orientated. "I think that sadly the Coronation Club turned into a bingo hall in all but name."

Joe Reynolds shared a similar view. "A lot of clubs were more like bingo halls by the 1980s but they did provide a lot of local musicians with work."

The meat raffle

Other little flutters were popular such as the raffles. Every club had regular ones and also one-offs for a particular charity or cause.

Prizes for raffles varied over the decades with bottles of spirits often the top prizes, knick-knacks or toiletries. Committee men would go around the club selling raffle tickets which were usually drawn the same evening or lunchtime.

Joints of meat started to appear as prizes from around the mid- 1970s when industrial decline and job losses hit the city hard. These were much more useful than knick-knacks or a bottle of scotch!

The "tote" (short for totalizer) was another way for the club to fundraise and for members to win something.

Games and sports were a central part of club life but placing and taking bets on any game in or outside the club, such as horse racing, was forbidden. There were strict rules about betting and clubs could be cast out of the CIU if caught allowing it on their premises.

Hen Lane stated this clearly in its rules, November 1963. "All known runners barred from the club during the hours of racing." Any person found taking bets would be in trouble with the committee. Such activities did sometimes go on, though, with a blind eye turned now and then.

At the Godiva British Legion, Paul Wortley used to notice the regulars who congregated around the TV in the bar and watched the horse racing. "They regularly went to speak with the doorman, nicknamed 'Sailor.' It wasn't until I noticed he had some sort of contraption akin to a bus conductor, in the doorman's alcove that I became aware that he worked for a 'bookie' and was responsible for taking bets. The contraption was some sort of time stamp machine I think!"

In general the low-level, highly regulated forms of gambling that members participated in was for fun, to earn some extra money or to enjoy some social life with friends.

Mr Walrus felt that if not for the Coronavirus lockdown in Spring 2020, his 95 year-old dad would still be going to Hen Lane club for Sunday bingo!

IT'S ALL FOR A **GOOD** **CAUSE** - CHARITIES, CHOIRS AND COMMUNITY

CHAPTER EIGHT ★

Binley Male Voice Choir

In the sweltering hot summer of 1976 Barras Green members were lining up to throw wet sponges at the club Secretary. They paid ten pence for the pleasure, with Vic Terry in the stocks and committee member Peter Baker taking a turn. The wet sponges might have been welcome but not the rotten tomatoes and lettuces!

It was all in aid of the Ace of Clubs charity that raised money nationally for the Muscular Dystrophy group. Barras Green organised various events over two weeks including a ladies' darts contest, collecting a grand total of £170.

Fundraising for good causes was part of the Working Men's Club tradition that Coventry clubs enthusiastically continued. The causes were wide-ranging, such as the CIU's convalescent homes, or a member's child in need of specialised medical care.

Helping out local communities was evident in many of the events and activities that clubs organised.

Coventry WMC was also one of the biggest supporters of the CIU convalescent homes. The committee thought up different ways to raise money, one being to allocate £1.50 from the weekly tote, which raised £483 between 1951-1961.

★ Did you know?
The CIU Convalescent Homes
Long before the welfare state, club convalescent homes were opened as places of recuperation for club members who had experienced sickness or surgery. The first one, Pegwell Bay in Kent, opened in 1894. The number of homes eventually rose to five with Langland Bay, Broadstairs, Saltburn and Grange-over-Sands added."

Radford Social ran free concerts for its 50th anniversary in 1969 but asked members for donations for the homes and its OAP fund.

At the Railwaymen's Club in late 1961 members packed into the concert room for a "great night" and to see President Les Arthur hand over three £100 cheques. These were for the Lord Mayor's Christmas fund for OAPs, Coventry Boys Club and the CIU homes.

In November 1961 Hen Lane Club held a raffle for the blind and the next month another in aid the Lord Mayor's appeal, a city-wide charity. In 1962, one of their fundraisers was a concert held in aid of the Muscular Dystrophy Group.

Many Coventry clubs supported another CIU charity - the Club Scribes. Established in 1901,

this raised money for blind club members across the country.

Cheylesmore Club fund-raised for many charities including Guide Dogs for the Blind. In September 1972 the club presented a cheque to Inspector Duffy of Coventry and Warwickshire Police. This was for the family of PC Guthrie who had been tragically killed whilst on duty in the city.

Coombe Social supported the Prostate Cancer charity and helped out members experiencing hard times. During the Falklands War, club member Sergeant Eric Watson was badly injured in the battle of San Carlos Bay.

Eric's father was a club member and official and along with the committee organised fund raising shows and raffles. On his return Eric was welcomed back with a special social event in his honour and presented with a cheque for £325. The concert featured popular local group Calvary.

Being sponsored for running marathons became popular after the first London Marathon in 1981. Many ran for charity often in daft costumes that made more difficult but attention grabbing. All sorts of wacky ways were adopted to part people from their cash!

There were also sponsored head shaves that raised thousands over the years.

You name it, Coventry's clubs and their members have done it when it comes to charities and good causes.

Langland Bay ex-convalescent home early 21st century

St. Stephens Church, Canley

Right: CIU Convalescent Homes

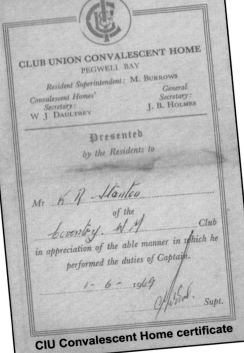

CIU Convalescent Home certificate

Reaching out to the community and a bit of culture!

Clubs provided not just entertainment but many cultural and community facilities and events.

Hen Lane's modern extensions in 1965 were planned to include something more traditional - a small library for its 2000 members.

"Packed in large boxes are the books, which will be used in the library. Twenty of the books are straight from publishers and donated by Mr. Maurice Edelman, MP."

It was expected that more books would be donated and shared. Club Secretary Bob Pattison said: "The original concept of the Working Men's Club - a community way of life for the working man and his family, is now being brought to full fruition. There is tremendous need for cultural as well as social activities and we believe that this new club image will do just that."

★ **Barry Meek:**
"I played in a band called the Internationals. Along with a band called the Barry John 5 we played a gig at Tile Hill Social to raise money for the first scanner at Walsgrave Hospital. There was the door money, raffle money and the people there thought that that was not enough so they got a bottle tub and half filled it with cash. Those were the days when Massey Ferguson, the Standard, Jaguar, Alvis and all the other industries were at their height. Good times!"

Trev Teasdel's mum used the Willenhall Social and he benefited one time from its informal book exchange. In 1975 he was doing a Social Studies course at local Henley College and Robert Tressell's Ragged-Trousered Philanthropists was course reading. Trevor wasn't sure where he'd get hold of a copy but got a nice surprise back home.

"My mother was in a number of book clubs and liked mostly romantic or historical novels. But I saw she had a copy of that very book! It turns out it was doing the rounds at Willenhall Club and someone passed it on to her."

A variety of cultural activities and amenities were found right across Coventry's clubs.

Several clubs had very accomplished male voice choirs. Wyken WMC's choir was established by founder member and Secretary George Winterburn. They travelled across the city, won many accolades and also raised money for charities.

Radford Social's choir was another, formed in 1946 by members on short-time working at the factories. They celebrated their coming of age on September 15th 1967. They won the Warwickshire CIU Music Festival on three occasions plus other trophies.

"While the choir's activities take them to all parts of the country, nothing gives them greater

pleasure than when they are giving their services voluntarily to charitable organisations within Warwickshire."

The men of Binley were enthusiastic singers as well as club goers. They joined forces with singers from Coombe Social and formed the Binley Male Voice Choir in 1946. The original ten members soon became 30 but Friday, 13th July, 1947 brought very bad luck indeed.

A tragic mining accident killed several choir members. The remaining ones immediately started organising concerts to raise money for the disaster fund.

The choir went from strength to strength after that, regularly taking part in competitions and appearing in many prestigious concerts across the country. They even performed with Paul Robeson, who appeared at the Coventry Hippodrome in the late 1950s.

If choirs were not your thing there was the occasional fashion show, such as the one put on at the Canley Social in 1963. This was a first for a CIU club. Out of 1200 members at Canley Club, 400 were women and many turned up on the day. The dresses were mainly from the Coventry Cooperative Society, which presented the show.

Early in 1965, the usual Sunday evening concert

★ **Estelle Brain:** "
Binley Miners' Working Mens' Club was in the pit village. Famous for its very popular Male Voice Choir, my dad and two uncles were members. The village had a large population of Welsh and Scottish families."

was replaced by something very different at the same club, a play put on by the city's celebrated Belgrade Theatre company. Maria Marten "went down well" with the members and they were soon asking the club's secretary when the company was coming back!

The actors saw it as a "wonderful success." The club was clearly a suitable venue for theatre, being used to hosting many forms of entertainment.

Community-focused Hen Lane held an exhibition of paintings by one of its members, Mr. Pelling, in November 1974.

In 1981, when industrial decline was hitting hard, the club held exhibition of local children's work

The Canley Club

<u>Free</u> Football on Mondays at the Canley Club

8yrs-12yrs 6.00pm-7.00pm
12yrs-16yrs 7.00pm-8.00pm

The Canley Club, Marler Road, (off Charter Avenue), Canley.

Telephone: Jim McCleave 07538089942

Football for all at the Canley Social

Rev Simon Stephens, a regular at Canley Social

making sure the parade went without a hitch and also showed what it meant to them."

The annual parade meant a lot to many others as well.

Even the bishop enjoyed a pint!

Not only did clubs reach out to local communities but those in the community sought to reach into the clubs to do their work. The Bishop of Warwick, Rt. Rev. Clive Handford, went knocking at the Wyken WMC's door in 1992 and he found it open.

He held three informal meetings there to discuss religious beliefs with club members. Two local vicars were also involved - Rev. Richard Worsley and Rev. Nigel Adams - who used the club regularly. They thought it made sense as the club was between their two churches. And the Bishop enjoyed a pint! He said he was "delighted to be there" and appreciated the hospitality.

Father Simon Stephens didn't wait at his church – which was oddly called St. Stephens - for people to come but went to meet his flock at the place they liked the best - the Canley Social! The popular vicar was quick to get involved in activities for local people centred around the club.

Father Simon enjoyed a pint and was bought one or two by members who appreciated him coming to the club and getting involved with them. He married some, christened their babies and performed funeral services.

Joe and Babs Lee were the club's steward and stewardess in the 1970s. Joe recalls how Simon Stephens married them for the second time. "Such a nice guy. A real humanist."

Until 1955, there was no church on the Canley estate though it had the club and a pub. The local bishop back then described the place as "godless"! But close links did develop between churches, schools and clubs across the city.

A short back and sides and a pint!

There was also a bit of a hair thing going on too! Getting to a barber's was not always easy for busy working men so some barbers had slots made available at clubs to cut their hair.

Barry Savage lived opposite the Canley Club and a neighbour was a trainee hairdresser. "On a Sunday morning he was allowed to cut gents hair in the club. Boosted his wages a little!"

Mark Rewhorn recalls that at Coombe Social members went in early doors Friday nights to get a cheap haircut. "The barber used one of the changing rooms for his temporary salon. By the time the missus arrived for her game of bingo, her man was neatly trimmed and usually three sheets to the wind!"

Coventry's clubs, with their large rooms and facilities, were first class venues not only for concerts but also for a wide range of community events and activities.

and ran a course on rights for senior citizens. These were a break in the usual club offering but relate to educational aims of the early club movement.

Never a club to stand still for long, the committee embarked on a series of "education shops" in 1983 including activities involving the local schools in the area.

The committee thought it would be good to bring teachers to the club for parents' evenings. With parents on "home territory" some found it much easier to talk about how their children's education. And teachers could enjoy a pint afterwards!

Hen Lane also provided a wide range of activities for members such as ladies keep fit classes, typing lessons and sewing classes.

The city's British Legion clubs also had community-oriented activities. Paul Wortley lived for several years at the Godiva Club in Spon Street.

"I grew up to understand the meaning of the work the British Legion did across the country. Watching the standard bearers practise their routines in the days before the Remembrance Day parade was a great insight. They put so much work put into

THE COCKLE MAN'S ARRIVED!
FOOD AND DRINK

CHAPTER NINE ★

Nothing better than a Faggot and Pea Batch... and a Beer!

Above: Carol busy getting ready for the faggot and pea batch rush at the Hatch!

"**Y**ou got crabs? Poor man had to put up with that every five minutes!" Chris Long was referring to the cockle man, of course!

He probably didn't have crabs but crabsticks were in his basket as well as best-selling packets of cockles and mussels.

A simple taste of the seaside in a city that couldn't be further away from the sea if it tried!

He'd open your packet, shake in some vinegar and give you a wooden stick. Dressed in a white coat he looked every bit the fishmonger as he did the club rounds.

★ **Barbara Weightman:**
"Cockles and potato crisps.
Plus we used to take sandwiches, can you imagine!"

Clubs hadn't been set up with the aim of feeding members. Working men would eat their tea at home after work and had little spare money for meals out in former times. But snacks were available in most clubs and much more as times got better and people had "never had it so good!"

A Batch from the hatch!

Tile Hill Social had its own Batch Bar recalls John D'Arcy and "the faggots and peas always went down well.'

Helen Reith had great insights into this Coventry delicacy, being recruited to the family's catering efforts from an early age. Grandparents Lillian and Sidney Pinker were steward and stewardess of the Canley Club in the 1960s.

"My Nan was famous for her faggot and peas, it was the 'best seller.' You could have them in a batch or in a bowl. You could also have just a cup of mushy peas which was quite popular. The queue used to go all the way down the concert room in the bingo interval!"

Mrs Pinker used to cook the faggots, peas and also pigs feet on a cooker behind the then concert room bar. Helen's mum Sylv later took up the batch baton.

"Between them they ran it for quite a few years. My sisters and myself all had to take our turn helping out. It was only open on bingo and concert nights. They also supplied the buffet for games night."

Get that tie straight!

Kath Hickey later ran the food hatch at the Canley Club. She is often described as "a legend" for making sure everyone got their interval food. Kath cooked her own pork for the pork and stuffing batches.

★ **Teresa Eyden Wycherley:**
★ "The Barras Green Club did memorable faggots and peas."

Hen Lane took its catering arrangements to a whole new level by having a restaurant and even a catering committee!

Below: CIU List of clubs 1959

Right: Radford Club's Menu for OAPs dinner

Phil Bunn, Hen Lane's Secretary, recalls the restaurant opening in the mid-1960s.

"It ran for a good few years. People were coming in on Sunday afternoon. It wasn't just about the food but the company as well. It would be people who didn't have anyone at home, just sitting at home on their own, who would come for their dinner. There would be 30 or 40 people up there. It was all about community then, helping people out."

Phil also recalls Hen Lane's first presentation for life members to mark the club's 25th anniversary. "Some of the food on offer! I don't think they'd get away with it nowadays! Loads there. Toasts to the Queen. All very proper."

Carol Stafford's dad had a dinner surprise at his club one evening.

"My dad really liked the Tile Hill Social. He spent LOT of time there! In fact my Mum delivered his dinner to him there one night- she actually threw it at him!"

Games nights usually involved food. A tea of some sort often preceded the games and sports presentations ceremonies.

Joanne Sweeney's mother in law, Winifred, was stewardess at the Tile Hill Social. "She always put on a great buffet and the football team loved her pies after a match."

Winifred also catered for many weddings and parties at the club. "She was always out of pocket as she wanted to make sure there was plenty of food for everybody!"

At the Godiva British Legion, Paul Wortley's stewardess mum organised the catering for games nights, weddings and other events.

On Sunday mornings most clubs usually laid on plates of cheese and crackers on the bar.

Canley not only had a food hatch but a tuck shop! For Nicola Crane it was "a great social leveller! It didn't matter if your parents had a little or a lot, we all had 10p for the tuck shop".

Not just any crisps but Robinson's crisps!

Robinson's crisps are a part of Coventry's history. The crisps were an offshoot of the Robinson family's fish and chip shop in Binley. Arthur Robinson started making the crisps in the late 1940s, after closing time. His wife, Bessie, would pack them up. A few neighbours were employed to help out as orders increased.

CLUBMEN!

drink

Club's Brewery Beers

Share the benefits of Co-operative Brewing

LOYALTY PAYS

APRIL 1959

LIST OF 3473 CLUBS

which are members of

THE WORKING MEN'S

Club and Institute Union

LIMITED

Club Union Buildings, 127 Clerkenwell Road, London, E.C.1

Telephone: HOLborn 5942

Explanation of Notes to List of Clubs
a—Club does not admit Associates
b—Club does not open on Sundays

The attention of Associates is drawn particularly to the Notes on page 4.

Menu

Soup

Roast Turkey, Pork

Creamed Potatoes, Sprouts, Peas

Apple Tart and Custard

or

Fruit and Cream

Toasts

THE QUEEN
PROPOSED BY
M. Phillips, Vice President

THE CLUB
PROPOSED BY
W. J. Prewett, President

THE GUESTS
PROPOSED BY
R. Pattison, Secretary

Mr Robinson would drive around the city's clubs and pubs to deliver the crisps, supplied in big tins with a distinctive, local logo: an image of Coventry's legendary three spires.

They were so popular that Arthur started to make them full time in a factory in the 1950s. Each bag contained that small pack of salt and each one made by Bessie's own hand! She also designed the crisp packet. It was a real family business that kept club goers happy until the national brands took over.

What's your tipple?

With so much going on in the clubs, it's a wonder members found time to get a round or two of drinks in. By the 1970s, most clubs had large rooms each with their own bar which were buzzing on busy nights.

Clubs were known to be cheaper places to drink than pubs. They supplied alcoholic refreshments to members with no landlord to take a profit. The aim was that what was made from the sale of drink went back into the club.

★ **Philip Sephton:**
★ "Mild for me, once I reached drinking age, of course!"

Double Diamond was a popular beer first brewed as India Pale Ale in Burton on Trent. Bottled Double Diamond was nationally distributed from the 1940s onwards and became one of the highest selling beers in the UK from the 1950s to 1970s.

Double Diamond ad

"We're only here for the beer—it's Double Diamond"

One ad claimed "it worked wonders". Another advertising campaign had the slogan "I'm only here for the beer" which was often repeated in Coventry's clubs!

Mitchells and Butlers (M&B) brewery helped slake many a thirst with their famous Brew XI - "brewed for the men of the Midlands."

By the 1970s drinking tastes were changing with clubs trying to keep up with the latest trends. Members didn't all desert former preferences but there was a lot more was on offer.

Lager really took off in 1970s. Hofmeister had their cool "follow the bear" campaign, which appealed to younger drinkers.

Above: A posh ' do' for Hen Lane Club!

THE ROYAL BRITISH LEGION

COVENTRY No. 1 MEN & WOMEN BRANCH

4th Annual DINNER & DANCE

Concert Room
BRITISH LEGION GODIVA
(COVENTRY) CLUB LTD.

on Friday, October 18th 1974

Chairman:
S. BRADBURY, Esq., Branch President

Godiva British Legion 4th Dinner and Dance

Former Fed Brewery on Torrington Ave

Clubs started stocking it along with other lagers such as Harp, which was "sharp till the bottom of the glass."

Sometimes the price decided the choice, especially when the city's workers were on strike or working short time.

John D'Arcy took a liking to lager and lime when he first started drinking at Tile Hill Social. "Fed lager was definitely cheaper. It probably helped that the brewery was situated on Torrington Avenue, near the Lime Tree Club. That cut down the haulage costs for sure!"

Bottom of Form

The "Fed", short for Northern Clubs Federation Brewery, was set up and run by a co-op of working men's clubs with a branch in the Midlands. It dates back to 1921 and the dissatisfaction not only at the shortages of beer but the practice of some breweries watering it down. The "Fed" supplied beer to clubs more cheaply than the commercial breweries.

Mark Rewhorn drank "whatever bitter was on tap." His dad preferred mild. Richard Harvey was also partial to mild but "livened it up with a bottle of Gold Label, which certainly added to the overall effect! " Gold Label was a brand of Barley Wine, Bass No 1 another. "Sold in 1/3 of a pint bottles. Definitely a 'winter warmer!'"

A welcome smile at the bar!

Paul Wortley remembers barmaid Elsie at the Godiva British Legion club who liked a barley wine. "I was unsure what it was at the time but now understand that it's basically dynamite in liquid form."

Another local brewery, Hook Norton, became involved in loaning clubs large sums of money for refurbishments. These were difficult to pay back when clubs started to go in decline.

Something for the ladies!

Women often drank the same things as men, though not in the same quantities! Some drinks were aimed at them with an appeal to sophistication, generally being more expensive. That was fine if the boyfriend was paying!

And what was it with all those drinks with a cherry on top?

★ **Helen Reith:**
★ "Brandy and Babycham, can't stand it now
★ though! And port and lemon, we all thought
★ we were so posh back then."

Babycham sold millions from the late 1950s into the 1970s. Their long running advertising campaign had a cute doe-eyed deer on the bottle and catch phrase- "Babycham, I'd love a Babycham!"

Susan Lowe was partial to Sweet Martini and lemonade, topped off with a cherry.

The 1970s saw drinks companies increasingly target women with new offerings for the younger generation.

Having a quick fag break! Barman Keith at Canley Social

Photo first, buffet second! Winning team at Canley Social

They'd turn their noses up at a bottle of milk stout - they wanted something more glamorous!

Meryl Barrett sometimes had a vodka and lime until she drank too much vodka! And she ''loved a snowball'', not the sort you chuck around in winter but those made from advocaat and lemonade, with the compulsory cherry!

Liz Smith liked a glass or two of cider. She was at the Builders Club to watch the memorable FA Cup of 1987 when Coventry City beat Spurs.

★ **Graham Johnson:**
★ "Cherry B for the ladies!"

"I remember that I got a bottle of special FA Cup commemoration beer! They gave them out to the regulars and it was a great memory of the day." She still has the bottle!

Wine? Not unheard of but few would be ordering that until foreign holidays to the Costas and beyond really took off.

Children had their own favourites. Lants "sparkling minerals" were sold in many clubs. As a child, Mark Rewhorn used to drink Lanto-"Lants version of Vimto."

Many children, including Patricia Coleman, loved a glass of Dandelion and Burdock.

For Nicola Crane, a trip to the Canley Club had

her licking her lips at the prospect of a lemonade and blackcurrant. Janice Lyn Lenton Denman, who called it "pink paraffin," was another fan.

Let's not forget the bar staff and glass collectors!

Norma Stephens started working at the Lime Tree club as soon as she turned eighteen.

"I worked in the snooker room and loved it. My granny was also the glass collector when she was in her 70s!"

Chris Mckirdy's children "all did their apprenticeship behind the bars, it was a great time!"

Paul Wortley's parents employed various people at the Godiva British Legion which was "a large and busy club at that time." He recalls barmaid Elsie being a "real character."

City FA Cup win M&B ad

Right: Liz Smith's FA Cup Commemoration beer 1987 vintage!

Leaving the bar behind-Margaret and Ken Cooper's wedding day

"I think Elsie was about 60 years old and had spent much of her life in and around the licensed trade. It's fair to say Elsie used 'industrial' language at times, in fact most of the time, when anyone who had consumed more alcohol than they should have done needed to be told they were leaving the premises. Not many dare argue with Elsie!"

Elsie would often be found with a cigarette balanced precariously in the corner of her mouth. Paul's dad had to "pluck up the courage" to tell her that she could only smoke in the car park around the back, not near the bar!

Margaret Cooper and husband Ken were bar staff at the Canley Social when they were saving for their wedding. "We worked on and off

behind the bar right up till 1979 when we emigrated to Australia."

Ian Greaves was never officially on the payroll at the Stoke Aldermoor club but through a friend who did some shifts behind the bar, worked there himself, around 1972/3.

"The steward told me I'd soon pick it up - on the job training I guess!"

Ian started on a bingo night. "We'd be doing nothing for a while and then everyone converged at the bar when a house was called. I was soon deemed to be ready for weekend shifts!"

He can still remember some of the prices: mild 10p a pint, bitter 12p and Tartan 13p with most shorts around 12p.

"It was great fun working at the bar on a busy night and there would be either live music or a disco at the weekends. The members were a friendly lot and there were always plenty of tips, which went into a pot to be divided out at the end of the night. I was paid about £2 a shift and we were allowed to have free drinks, in moderation- draught beer or soft drinks."

Once the bar closed, the bar manager would let them go and have a dance in the concert room. "This was very popular with us all, the only condition was that we still had to clear up at the end of the night, after which we could relax together over a last drink. I felt like I was being paid for enjoying myself!"

Glass collecting in many clubs was a job often done by either young people or older members. It was part time work, a bit of money and also company in a place people probably would have been going to anyway!

Whiteways drinks ad for Clubs

Canley Social's Jimmy Cooke helps out behind the bar

"BE NOT FORGETFUL TO **ENTERTAIN STRANGERS**."

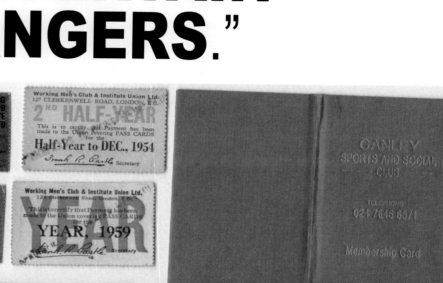

CHAPTER TEN

Pass cards

Here's a question: "If a foreigner asked you to show him British social life at its best, where would you take him?"

The answer? To a Working Men's Club!

So began an article in the September 1970 edition of the CIU's monthly journal. The reasons given included to witness the democracy of club life in action, with members deciding for themselves about the facilities, food, drink and quality of the services.

Another reason was the tolerance of clubs, with members sometimes disagreeing but not becoming embittered. The great social life clubs provided was mentioned. The article stated: "A man's club is an extension of his home, particularly with the great influx of family membership in recent years. Your club is a neighbourly place. It is your place, in the sense that you are as much the owner as any other members."

★ **Nick Edgington:** "Me and the wife were on holiday in Benidorm one year and the hotel waiter asked us where we were from. When I told him Coventry, he said, 'Ah, Cox Street Club!' He had friends had taken him there. He'd clearly been impressed."

Coventry's clubs were neighbourly places and most people knew each other. Over the decades Coventry's clubs welcomed many visitors from near and far and showed respect to the CIU's motto:

"Honour all men, love the brotherhood, use hospitality one to another, be not forgetful to entertain strangers and he that need have friends must himself be friendly."

Some clubs were established by newcomers to the city, such as Hen Lane Club and those founding members from the Rhondda. There were

considerable contributions from Geordies who had come to Coventry during the war, bringing with them their skills and a strong club-going tradition. Many Scots and Irish also made Coventry their home, adding their culture and traditions to club life.

★ **Joe Reynolds:**
★ "Some clubs were good, some were bad,
★ some unfortunately had these 'colour bars'.
★ I remember pickets outside the Barras
★ Green Club. Some of the better clubs
★ were Stoke Ex-Servicemen's, the Lime
★ Tree and Tile Hill clubs."

After the war, Polish, Lithuanian and Italians were among many migrants who settled in Coventry. They helped to rebuild the city and also to establish Working Men's Clubs. Willenhall Social was one such club whose members had diverse origins but shared a common aim of having the best club they possibly could.

Coventry's clubs were praised for their international links, being keen to make connections across the world. Given the strong trade union links of clubs, this was seen as a normal course of action.

In 1965 Canley Social Club hosted the Rozmarynka Orchestra from Prague with the audience "most appreciative" of the change in routine. The orchestra was supported by the Wyken WMC Male Voice Choir. Club Secretary Mr. Jimmy Cooke spoke of the standing ovation, the like of which he had never witnessed in the club before.

The visit was arranged by the Coventry Committee for International Understanding and emphasized the advantages of CIU affiliated clubs. The visitors were "greatly impressed" by the club and its facilities as their own were more industry based.

Willenhall Social Club hosted a delegation of shop stewards and trade union officials from Hamburg in 1970. They were greeted by the club's President, Tom Ferguson after a twelve-day study tour of local factories.

The club visit was intended to give some insights into the social life of the city's workers, with the Working Men's Clubs right at its centre. Hamburg did not have the tradition of Working Men's Clubs though there were a number of sports clubs.

This delegation was of special significance because great efforts were being made to promote reconciliation and friendship between Coventry

SOUL SMILE: Ray King

GROUP MAKE AN INSTANT HIT

Rush release hits 'A' side

FOLLOWING soul legend Ray King's induction into the Coventry Music Wall of Fame, Telegraph contributor Pete Clemons looks back on his career. Rock fan Pete, who lives in Keresley, is currently compiling an archive of the Coventry music scene.

SHARING STAGES: (above) Ray King played alongside Bill Haley and Jimi Hendrix; **(left)** Ray singing with Neol Davies

Pioneering Ray King- tackled discrimination head on!

Coventry Soul band Stax

STAX

and German cities that suffered devastation during the war.

In the mid-1980s, clubs played host to visitors from their twin city of Jinan in China, which was just beginning to open up to the West. Delegations of Chinese Communist Party members were shown around clubs, given club ties and pins and probably treated to a pint of beer. Such clubs did not exist in China.

There are many other instances that show how Coventry clubs welcomed visitors from overseas. But there were also times quite the reverse happened.

The story of Coventry's first professional black singer, Ray King, illustrates what was happening in some clubs in the 1960s and early 1970s.

Ray, whose real name is Vibert Cornwall, was born in St. Vincent in the Caribbean and arrived in Coventry in 1963. His ambition was to become a singer and in achieving that he became a bit of a mover and shaker on Coventry's music scene. He worked the local club circuit and gained local fame before being offered work at top London venues and invited to do international tours.

His talent and charisma even influenced Coventry's pioneering 2 Tone bands such as the

Specials. Just as 2 Tone confronted racism and showed how people could come together, Ray King's personal rise to fame involved confronting racial discrimination in a few Coventry clubs.

When he entered a singing competition at the Edgewick Trades Hall club, he had heard the club was known to operate what was then called a "colour bar." He arrived on the night with his stage clothes and companion but the doorman wasn't sure about letting him in even though he was in the competition.

The Entertainment Secretary saw that Ray's name was indeed on the list. With some reluctance he took him in up to the changing room and told him to wait there till it was his

German Delegation visit Coventry Club

turn. Ray had not only made it into the club but went on to win the competition!

During one interview he spoke of how he decided to add a rendition of Harry Belafonte's Banana Boat Song, as a bit of a dig about the reluctance to stop him entering the club.

By the time Ray had been booked for a concert at Barras Green club, he had gained local fame and a strong fan base so could pull in a crowd. Once again he found it hard to get in. The doorman stopped him and the Entertainment Secretary backed him up. Ray wasn't allowed to play at his own gig.

★ Alan Charles:

"The Barras Green club was infamous for operating a colour bar. Quite unbelievable nowadays but their rights as a private members club were even upheld by the House of Lords.

This incident led to a number of protests against this club and the "colour bar" policy in general. Ray King was popular and his fans wanted to hear him sing. They also wanted racial discriminatory practices to end so that any one wanting to join and use the local clubs, no matter the colour of their skin or where they came from, could do so.

It wasn't only in Coventry where some clubs were operating discriminatory practices with other cases coming to light in London and Preston.

The CIU National Executive stressed the right of clubs to run themselves. In1961 they stated that the CIU was non-political and non-sectarian, as was each of its affiliated clubs. Such matters were meant for each individual club committee to decide in the best interests of the club and its members.

In their desire to avoid dictating policy to clubs, they came across as implicitly supporting clubs that discriminated against ethnic minorities. The CIU Executive seemed to sit on the fence with a failure to condemn the practice outright.

Below: Tremlett's History of the CIU

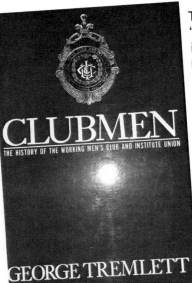

CIU historian George Tremlett believed it had made "a serious error of judgment in the controversial field of race relations".

Whilst the CIU upheld their "welcoming strangers" motto they simultaneously upheld the right of each club to decide for themselves, as private member's clubs, their own entry policy.

It was also pointed out that any would-be members had to be proposed, seconded and accepted. A club member who held a CIU Pass Card could

be allowed to visit other clubs but entry ultimately depended on those clubs.

In the 1970s, with a growing body of legislation in place, it became more urgent to sort out this issue for once and for all. The plea by those clubs who turned away potential visitors and members because of the colour of their skin that integration over time is better than being forced by legislation sounded lame.

Some also believed that politicians telling clubs what to do through legislation would not make them accept a more diverse membership.

Change came slowly in some clubs whilst it was happening quickly in society at large. Those clubs that did discriminate looked very out of step with the times. Younger members in particular shunned them and there were some protests and boycotts by members against discrimination. Some clubs lost members who simply took their custom elsewhere.

Ray King was welcomed into many other Coventry clubs such as the Walsgrave WMC where he first performed with the Ray King Soul Band in 1966. Ray, who made Coventry his home, went from strength to strength.

By the 1980s, much had changed and it was not unusual to see more diversity in club membership, on the committees as well as on the stage.

Joe Reynolds and Bob Drury were members of the soul band Stax that played at pubs and clubs in the early 1980s. When vocalist Carol Lloyd left the band she was replaced for a while by none other than Ray King. A member of The Selecter, Desmond Brown also joined them briefly. Joe had played saxophone on The Selecter's hit Three Minute Hero.

Those clubs that had been on the wrong side of social and cultural change, and potentially the law, had to accept the what was happening and adapt in order to survive.

The Barras Green Club closed down in 1982 having built up massive debts. It was sold to a group of 22 Indian factory workers and public transport employees who "chipped in" just like in the past to buy the gutted building from Whitbread Brewery. They reopened it as a community centre with many activities going on in the previous club such as Christmas parties for pensioners and music concerts.

By the early 1980s club committees as well as memberships were starting to reflect more the diverse nature of the city.

By the mid-1980s the Edgewick Trades Hall had been sold and been turned into an Indian community centre.

In 2010, Ray King, the singer who had provided a role model for many other musicians and entertainers was awarded an Honorary Degree from Coventry University.

MANAGING THE CLUBS
- PAST, PRESENT AND FUTURE

CHAPTER ELEVEN

★

Binley Club Committee

The club committee was a force to be reckoned with. Anyone who broke the rules would be "up on a charge" before you could say bingo. The "trial" usually took place before the bar opened at (high) noon, Sunday morning.

The military style language is understandable given that many committee members saw active duty during the war. They were a tough bunch, some having survived heavy fighting, forced marches and prison camps.

Wrong-doers had to account for their behaviour or else! They might be barred for a few weeks or, much worse - permanently. That would be like being cast out of Eden! A minor infringement would bring a "severe reprimand and warning" but being allowed back on probation.

To make matters worse, those barred would find their names published on the "naughty list" in the

★ **Roy Lenton:**
★ "God help you if you ever voted against the committee and club secretary!"

CIU's own monthly journal. A very public form of naming and shaming!

Whilst brawling and betting could get a member into trouble, so could rudeness. A Hen Lane Club member was on a "charge of misconduct" in June 1964, for knocking over two glasses of gin and orange and for refusing to pay for them to be replenished. "The miscreant was suspended."

The club committee, the elected body that managed the club, managed the members as well. This brought praise from politicians and the police.

When opening Hen Lane's new concert room in 1964, Lord Mayor Alderman Mrs Emily Allen summed up it nicely.

Tile Hill Social Committee

"Working Men's Clubs are an example of self-government by all. You organize your clubs, elect your own officers. It is similar to local councils where we represent you."

The local police was grateful for how committees nipped potential trouble in the bud.

Members voted onto the committee took on largely volunteer roles. A lot of time and responsibility were involved but many committee members remained in post for 20 years or more!

Members sometimes criticized those who looked to be entrenched, enjoying the power and the perks. But most club members didn't want to take on the onerous duties and left them to get on with it.

The CIU Club Journal discussed this in May 1970. "The running of a club is a highly skilled operation. Those who serve are all playing their part. Often they receive nothing except complaints when something goes wrong."

Long-serving committee members received CIU certificates at special presentation ceremonies. Les Arthur joined the Railwaymen's Club committee in 1941 and carried out various duties for 30 years. This was not untypical as some continued to do committee work well into their later years.

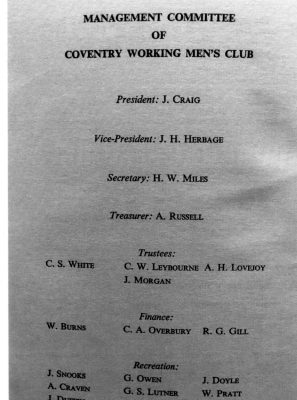

MANAGEMENT COMMITTEE
OF
COVENTRY WORKING MEN'S CLUB

President: J. CRAIG

Vice-President: J. H. HERBAGE

Secretary: H. W. MILES

Treasurer: A. RUSSELL

	Trustees:	
C. S. WHITE	C. W. LEYBOURNE A. H. LOVEJOY	
	J. MORGAN	

	Finance:	
W. BURNS	C. A. OVERBURY	R. G. GILL

	Recreation:	
J. SNOOKS	G. OWEN	J. DOYLE
A. CRAVEN	G. S. LUTNER	W. PRATT
J. DUFFIN	J. CHATER	T. KENNY

Coventry WMC Committee names

★ **Wayne Millward:**
"The nights at the Canley Social Club with bands or comedians were great. I remember the control box that the committee man went into to operate the lights and sound."

Sub-committees were formed for special projects in some clubs with general duties such as calling and checking bingo, selling raffle tickets and making announcements.

Bending the rules wasn't beyond some committees, now and then!

Club entertainer Lee Ross remembers how at certain clubs "you could guarantee a 'lock in' after closing time." Those in the know would stay behind for a few after-hours drinks.

"I recall a few times when we would get the whisper early on in the night, usually Saturday or holidays, with the suggestion from the Ent Sec that we 'might want to leave the gear here tonight.' It was all really nod and a wink sort of stuff. I know many bands took advantage of it, rolling home by taxi when the sun came up."

On some occasions members taking in and consuming their own drink was overlooked though usually forbidden. It was New Year's Day at the Canley Social as Steve Cooke recalls.

"It was a day when my dad, who was Club Secretary, allowed people to bring a bottle from home and he would turn a blind eye. Great fun!"

Helen Reith has similar memories. "Members were allowed to take their own little bottle of spirits and have a toast with their pals. There would be bottles of whiskey passed around."

The Hogmanay tradition of having a "wee dram" with friends was honoured and took precedent over the law!

The steward and stewardess

The everyday running of the club - including managing bar and cleaning staff - fell to the steward and stewardess. These were paid posts, often live-in, so suited married couples.

Tile Hill Social had the well-liked Thomas and Winifred Sweeney at the helm for over 25 years. Joanne Sweeney remembers them "working all hours, the place being packed full at weekends. They literally lived and breathed the place as they lived on the premises."

Joanne should know - she married their son!

Tom Sweeney was so good at his job that he got offered another when on the club outing! John

Below: Hen Lane Club ballot paper

HEN LANE AND DISTRICT SOCIAL CLUB AND INSTITUTE

Ballot Paper

Friday & Saturday, September 23rd & 24th, 1966

Committee (7) required

	SPACE FOR X
W. BROWN	
G. GANE	
A. HOLLAND	
F. HURST	
W. KENNY	
J. McLAUGHLIN	
D. J. MORGAN	
W. R. MORRIS	
E. O'NEAL	
J. ROTHERY	
D. WILLIAMS	
J. J. WARD	
W. WAUGH	
O. WRIGHT	

Canley Social Club Committee on tour!

CIU's Derek Dormer presenting an award to Jimmy Cooke

D'Arcy tells how the club ran its trip to Seaton in the September break.

"There was a CIU club in the town that most of the parents used. Tom was offered the job as steward by their committee, such was his popularity, even among virtual strangers!"

Joe and Babs Lee were the Canley Social's live-in couple in the 1970s. "My wife Babs and I moved from Sheffield, with two kids, and really didn't know what to expect from people with different accents and attitudes! We were immediately accepted, feeling at home from day one. We made many friends, some are still friends to this day."

At the Godiva British Legion, Paul Wortley's parents were the steward and stewardess when the club moved to Spon Street in 1970. The family's living accommodation was on the second floor.

Paul recalls the ups and downs of growing up in

Joe and Babs Lee- steward and stewardess at Canley Social in the 1970s

a club.

"The life of a young person living in licensed premises could be lonely at times as your parents were both working a great deal of the time. Early start for dad cleaning the beer pipes, stocking the bars, ordering barrels and bottles of beer."

The upside? He soon became proficient at both snooker and bagatelle!

Jeffrey and Margaret Woodward between

★ **Chris Mckirdy:**
★ "My grandad was chairman of Coundon
★ Club. I met my husband in Bell Green
★ Club where his dad became full time
★ secretary and his brother was steward."

them spent more than 100 years helping out at Baginton's British Legion Club. They took on just about every role at the club including as stewards before finally retiring in 2011. Jeffrey said: "It's been a hugely important part of our lives."

For Hen Lane club's Secretary Phil Bunn,

★ **Mark Rewhorn:** "The Foleshill Club was
★ robbed one NYE whilst we were all in the
★ concert room seeing the New Year in. The
★ whole evening's takings gone!"

working for the club runs in the family. "I'm the third generation of my family to work here. The tall lad behind the bar, my son, is the fourth! My grandfather, Leonard Price, was a founder member. My dad was treasurer here, a bar steward, on the committee for 30 odd years. I've done committee work for 20 years."

Hen Lane's cleaning staff team was large enough in the 1970s to require a forewoman! That level of staff seems hard to imagine now as most clubs have downsized with a few people doing just about everything.

The cleaning ladies were the unsung heroines of the club. They'd go round with their mops, polish

★ **Rick Hough:**
★ "There were years when the life seemed
★ to have been sucked out of the clubs.
★ Unemployment and deprivation struck."

and dusters every day to get all the rooms spic and span!

They enjoyed nights out at the club but knew they'd be emptying their own ash trays the next day!

There were a few cases of stewards robbing the club that employed them. Walsgrave WMC's steward in 2013 took £7,000 from the safe and blew it all on drinking and gambling in Skegness.
Managing change

Clubs were managed on a model that evolved in the 19th century and as the 20th century progressed seemed overly bureaucratic, with too many rules and regulations. Managing clubs became harder as the older generation stepped down and the legal framework changed rapidly.

The absence of women was a long-standing issue. "Lady members" weren't eligible for committee roles. Regular attempts to change that ruling were defeated at the CIU annual general meetings. Coventry clubs that were CIU affiliated, the majority in the 1970s, had to obey these national decisions.

Change finally came in 2007 but long before then, necessity led to women taking on committee roles as social and economic changes began to impact negatively on clubs.

Women were seen selling bingo tickets and even calling the numbers. Fewer male volunteers increased the acceptance of women holding positions of responsibility.

Radford Club had Pat Sunner as Vice President for over 12 years and saw women become more active and gain more status over that period. Change was frustratingly slow and probably cost clubs many potential members, as well as income.

No social institution is free of "bad apples" and a few clubs were unfortunate to have dishonest committee members. Clubs could be an easy target for those wanting to help themselves.

Minor cases of fraud did occur, sometimes something more major and outright robberies. Most committee members were honest and diligent but sadly a few caused major damage to club finances and reputations.

Clubs started to go into decline even during the mid-1970s when they looked to be top of their game. Many committees couldn't see what was coming back then. They had been ambitious about extending and modernizing, some were still taking on big loans from banks and the breweries, believing that the crowds would just keep on coming.

In 1974, the rate of inflation was the highest the UK had ever seen. Clubs had to pay more for goods and services whilst members had less spending money in their pockets to spend. The prospects for 1975 weren't much better.

There was rapid industrial decline and growing unemployment in the city. Coventry's main industry, car production, started to fail and eventually there were complete plant closures. The economic fall-out was disastrous.

The city became, as the Specials sang in 1981, a "ghost town." The lyrics referring to clubs being closed down were just as relevant to Working Men's Clubs as the night clubs.

Keresley Coronation Club and Institute Ltd.

Lady Member's Card

Ladies Name:

Mrs. N EDGINGTON

No: 427

Entrance Fee £3.00

Members must produce their cards when requested

Secretary: J. McCluskey

Above: Lady Member's Card

Coventry's Industrial decline

A special dinner at the Canley Social

Production halved at BL car factories

Coventry Stewards Association trip to the Guinness Brewery

Hen Lane Committee

Members spent less time and money in their clubs. The once packed rooms started to empty and this put off younger members who now had other leisure options. The tradition of following their father's footsteps into club membership didn't appeal any more.

Committees found it hard to balance the books and to cope with increasingly complex laws around health and safety, gambling, equality and diversity. Many were not trained in these areas so no surprise that fewer members put themselves forward for the task. If loans were called in, clubs simply folded.

By the early 1980s, Edgewick Trades Hall was struggling badly. The local newspaper contrasted it to nearby Parkstone Club, which was doing well. "Two clubs barely half a mile apart experiencing widely different fortunes".

Crippled with losses, Edgewick Trades Hall members decided to sell the club. This story became all too common.

It became too expensive to open the large, once luxurious, concert rooms. It's ironic that many clubs that began in small huts retreated to using the smallest rooms for bingo and concerts. Often concerts were replaced by free 'n' easies or karaoke.

Many clubs tightened their belts and hung on into the new century but finally closed for the last time, no longer viable in a rapidly changing society.

The once very close relationship between Coventry's clubs and local politicians declined as the decades passed. Clubs could no longer look to them for praise or practical support, now viewed as businesses and not places at the heart of local communities.

The smoking ban is often blamed for the demise of clubs. But that didn't come till 2007 by which time many clubs had already closed. Mr Walrus believes: "Massive cultural change and drinking at home, especially wine, has really killed them off.

Hen Lane's much missed President Ray Baxter

Ray Baxter Club President 1983 - 2009

Meeting card for Coventry CIU Secretaries' Association

CIU HQ, Upper Street, London

Spot the Moustache! John Reynolds CIU Warwickshire branch President at an awards ceremony at the Canley Social

ROYAL BRITISH LEGION "GODIVA COVENTRY" CLUB LIMITED

At an Extraordinary General Meeting of the Members of the above-named Society, duly convened and held on 26th February 1984, the following Special Resolution was duly passed:

"That the Society be wound up voluntarily and Kenneth Sankey, of Park House, Station Square, Coventry CV1 2NS, be and is hereby appointed Liquidator for the purpose of such winding-up."

SF (186)
R. J. Hamilton, Chairman

Lime Tree Club Committee

Godiva British Legion closure

Shame really because they are still a good night out and far safer than many pubs."

Deregulation of licensing laws enabled supermarkets to sell alcohol cheaply so staying in became the new going out. There were more home-based activities as well, first videos then DVDs, computers and the internet.

Coventry clubs that survive still offer the amenities, activities and the community values that made them so unique. They may be operating on a reduced scale but continue to try different ways to keep members old and new coming through the doors.

People still need social life and recreation, a chance to meet with others in a social space that feels comfortable. Going to clubs has been increasingly acknowledged as an aid to reducing social isolation. They provide support and social life, familiarity and a bit of fun with friends.

We probably now need the clubs more than ever before.

A cleaner's work is never done!

Getting things cleaned up at the Canley Social!

CLUB JOURNAL
THE PAPER FOR ALL C.I.U MEMBERS
C.I.U

60p

Academic says community venues should be supported

STRUGGLING CLUBS NEED PUBLIC MONEY

A LEADING academic has called for public money to be used to help struggling clubs.

Dr Ruth Cherrington, who is writing a book on the history of clubs in Coventry, made the appeal after the closure of one of the Union's oldest clubs, Coventry WMC.

"Its closure is particularly sad because it is an iconic club," said Dr Cherrington. "In the past Coventry City Council was very supportive of working men's clubs because they were a part of the community. But now there seems to be no account for history and heritage.

"Clubs still provide services for people, particularly older people. So, where are these people going to go now?"

Coventry WMC was founded in 1862, the same year as the CIU, and was visited by The Queen in 1977, her Silver Jubilee year. It

closed last month with debts of £26,000 after an appeal to the High Court failed to buy extra time to raise funds.

"It wasn't a huge amount of money that the club owed. I do feel that the City Council or another body could have helped them out.

"Working men's clubs are a very big part of British heritage and they should be saved.

"Many can't run by themselves any more and need help from local councils or sponsors to try to make them more attractive again. If we don't do something now, we're likely to see more closures."

Dr Cherrington, who works at the Centre for Translation and Comparative Cultural Studies at the University of Warwick, was featured in the June *Club Journal* where she discussed her research into clubs in Coventry. She can also be heard on a University podcast on: www2.warwick.ac.uk/newsandevents/audio/

Richard just keeps on rocking

CLUBMAN Richard Theobald has proved you're never too old to rock 'n' roll by winning a talent contest at the age of 69. Richard will now be travelling to Blackpool in November for the semi-finals and final of the Pontin's Starquest talent competition. The winner will win the chance to record a five-track album as a professional recording studio.

Richard used to enter talent competitions when he was a teenager and took up singing again when karaoke became popular 20 years ago. In this year's finals he will be singing one song, his version of Buddy Holly's "Oh Boy!"

A big fan of Elvis Richard is one of the few people to see Buddy Holly when he toured Britain in 1958. A retired painter and decorator, he is a member of the Great Horton WMC in Bradford, but has moved to Bridlington, where he hopes to join the Victoria Sailors Club.

As well as singing Richard has won cups for his jiving and his talent has been passed on to his granddaughter Faye, who is appearing in the final of another Pontin's competition singing Whitney Houston's "I wanna dance with somebody".

Bob calls it a day at 90

FORMER prisoner of war Bob Dudley has finally retired at 90 after 25 years as a doorman at a Northamptonshire club.

When Irchester WMC was looking for a doorman it chose Bob over younger candidates because of his experience and mental toughness he had developed over five years as a PoW. His no-nonsense approach made sure nobody who was not a member got past without producing their Associate and Pass Cards.

"We employed Bob because he had a bit of charisma," said Club President Clifford Bates. "If he tells them to leave they go, no one takes any umbrage with him."

Bob started work at 14, joined the Army at 20 and was captured at Dunkirk. During his five years as a prisoner he had to rely on Red Cross parcels and fight against boredom and depression.

Bob Dudley

INSIDE...
News ... 2, 5, 7, 10, 14, 18
Charity races
SEDGEFIELD Racecourse
Westminster Words
Education
Crossword
Holiday & Convenience

AND A FEW MORE MEMORIES BEFORE YOU GO!

Why were the announcements so loud at the Boilermakers Club?

Alan Charles remembers going to the Boilermakers Club with his dad one day as a young lad. "When the Tannoy announced that there would be three houses of bingo, I nearly leapt out of my skin as it boomed out at terrific volume. I was quite scared, I'd never heard such a bossy voice at such volume. My dad laughed and said he should have warned us that as it was the Boilermakers the members were nearly all deaf as a result of their work. What a terrible thing!"

Carol Evatt spent "a large part" of her life down the Lime Tree. "We used to go every Friday, Saturday and Sunday lunchtime, occasionally Sunday night. My Mum always went on Tuesday night for the bingo as well!" Her mum was one of the first lady members at the Lime Tree and her Dad was on the committee at times and also

★ Did you know?
*The Radford Club's motto is
"My club is just what I make it."
This was on a sign that used to hang above the stage until the concert room was altered some years back.*

★ Alan Charles:
"The Barras WMC had a huge number of snooker tables and regularly hosted celebrity events where the best club players got a match with such stars of the day as Ray Reardon, Cliff Thorburn, even Hurricane Higgins. Incredible to be able to have the chance of seeing, let alone play against such celebrities."

used to make the posters advertising what was going to be on!

April Stephens' remembers helping her mum clean the snooker tables at the Tile Hill club. They had to be very careful with those treasured facilities! Tracy Perry Stokes' mum was a cleaner over at the Lime Tree Club. "I collected glasses in 1979, that's where I met my husband whose family still go there and play bingo!"

Anita Roden loved the Lime Tree Club parties that she went to with her brother. "They were a great treat and we were give ten shillings in an envelope!" Her father, John Lake, was Entertainment Secretary for some time at Tile Hill Social and grandad Tom looked after the 'cloaks' there for many years.

Above: Guess who'll be emptying those ash trays? Canley Social's cleaning ladies

Alan Charles recalls club outings to Drayton Manor Park for the club outings. Children would have a fist full of tickets for free rides and a nice sit down lunch later in the day. "One club pushed the boat out one year an took us to then embryonic Alton Towers. Star attractions - the cable car and pagoda fountain! He also remembers the Radford and London Road Clubs had kids parties every

★
★ **Carol Evatt:** "As kids going to the Lime Tree Club we used to make our own bingo cards and play along with the adults - packet of crisps if we won!"
★

year, held in their function rooms. "You could stuff yourself on pop, crisps and all the cheese or spam sandwiches you could eat. You got a really good gift after it all."

And the treats just kept on coming he says! "Every Christmas there would be a trip to the panto at the Coventry Theatre (Hippodrome), with a selection box to go home with. Luxury indeed! I got to see some of the biggest stars on TV at the time- Ken Dodd, Billy Dainty, Beryl Reid."

Spotting the young Elvis Costello at a Cox Street Club shop window!

Alan Charles was taken to the Cox Street club one Sunday morning, before opening time when they held a shop window. All the Entertainment Secretaries of Coventry WMCs were there to watch performers present their turns, hoping they would get signed for a gig at a later date.

"There was a name I recognised, Ross McManus, who had been a singer on the Light Programme and with the Joe Loss Orchestra. He sang covers of Beatles and other Merseybeat songs. It was a shame to see once-proud singers having to do this to get a living.

He had the help of a geeky-looking teenaged assistant operating a primitive light show for him- his son Declan.

Obviously influenced by his dad being on the music scene Declan followed in his footsteps. Re-invented as Elvis Costello, he went on to write and sing some of the most unforgettable songs of my era!"

Those faggot and peas batches!

Anita Roden was also a big fan of Tile Hill Club's "excellent food hatch with the best faggot and pea batches in town." Tracey Perry Stokes also remembers those tasty batches when she was at the Tile Hill Club with her granny.

Being a barman at the Barras!

Aged 17 and still at school, Alan Charles fibbed about his age to land a great Saturday job at Stoke Ex-Services club paying "the incredible wealth of six bob an hour!" He felt very naïve for not knowing there was mild ale- he'd only ever heard his dad order bitter! Once he could pull a proper pint, he was lured over to the Barras WMC where they paid a tanner an hour more!

We can just about squeeze in the Eastern Green Social Club, which dates back to 1958. Plans were submitted to Meriden District Council as the land lay just outside the Coventry boundary. Known locally as "the Green", it was seen as a Coventry club being very near to the Eastern Green and Tile Hill estates as well as the huge Massey Ferguson tractor factory.

April Stephens' dad was a founder member of this club. "My parents were also members of Tile Hill Social and later myself and ex-husband joined. Spent many good nights in both clubs!"

Acknowledgements

Kevin Smyth- former General Secretary of the CIU
For information, support and a sense of humour: members of
the Dirty Stop Outs Guide to 1970s Coventry, We Loved the
Canley Club, Coventry Old and New, True Coventarian, Albany
Social, Willenhall Social Club and Tile Hill Wood Facebook
Groups, Historic Coventry Forum and Bob Arnott.

Visuals:

Sheila Bates
Stuart Beamish
Lynda Bean Welch
Estelle Brain
Phil Bunn
Michael and Peter Cant
Steve Cooke
Margaret Cooper
Bob Drury
Sylvia French
Joe Lee
Toni Letts
Sandy Majhu
Jan Mayo
Chris Mckirdy

Debbie and Dean Nelson
Lorraine Pead
Tricia Pearson
Judith Peters
Helen Reith
Marion Reith
Joe Reynolds
Trev Teasdel
Dave Wassell
Linda Anne Wolohan
Paul Wortley
Teresa Eyden Wycherly

*And to all my family and
friends! Apologies if I've
left anybody out.*

Ruth and her dad having a good time at the Canley Social Club

The Author

Ruth Cherrington grew up across the street from the Canley Social club and from a very tender age enjoyed the family fun on offer there. After leaving Coventry, studying and working in Higher Education for over 30 years, she never forgot her roots and Coventry's clubs. This book fulfills a long-held ambition to tell their story as well as some of their many members. Ruth is the author of Not just Beer and Bingo! (Authorhouse 2012) and two Dirty Stop Outs Guides to Coventry. She has written articles and blogs on Coventry social history and culture and also set-up the Club Historians website - **www.clubhistorians.co.uk**